THE JOURNEY FROM **FEAR TO LOVE** IS SHORTER THAN YOU *THINK*

Nanci,
Embrace your power
& Live in Love
Susan D. Goudy

By

Susan D. Wedgewood-Goudy, MSW

Published by:
Pathway to Freedom Publishing
12643 Highland Oaks Place
Colorado Springs, CO 80921
Phone: 719-418-6698
www.journeyfromfeartolove.com

ISBN: 978-0-9853339-0-4

Library of Congress Control Number: 2012907802

Printed in the United States of America

For my dad-
Gordon Leigh Wedgewood

Who always believed in me

Table of Contents

Acknowledgments

A counselor/friend I knew many years ago, Pat Telford, once told me who I was as a person had everything to do with the journey I had taken in my life, prior to and including the day when we sat together talking. This meant that everything I had ever done—good, bad, or indifferent, every relationship I had ever been in, and all my encounters—had contributed to who I was. *I am who I am because of all of my life experiences*; therefore, it is impossible for me to show my appreciation to every single person who has contributed to the writing of this book (*Journey*). I'm grateful for the journey I have taken to get here and I thank all the people I have encountered along the way and appreciate all of my experiences.

I would like to thank my parents and my siblings. I would also like to thank my wonderful husband, my children, and my dogs. My husband and children have continually encouraged me to publish *Journey* and get moving on the next few books. My dogs have always shown me how to enjoy life. My friends have also continued to encourage me. Both family and friends have endured listening to me tell the story of the day I would publish *Journey*. Debbie Teiman read the first six chapters in their unedited form and gave it rave reviews, and without knowing it, with her enthusiasm, gave me the push I needed to get the book done. I would also like to thank all of the teachers I have had throughout my life, three of which have endorsed this book: Dr. Bruce Lipton (and his partner Margaret Horton), Rob Williams, and Stephen Lewis. Anita Kushen, who was my agent when I first put the book "out there," and Irene Lucas, who was my editor, are two others I wish to express my gratitude to. My nephew, Josiah Wedgewood, is an artist out of Nashville, Tennessee, and his beautiful artwork is the background for the cover of this book. I love you, Josiah, and thank you from the bottom of my heart for your contribution to the journey. I would also like to thank Brad Metzgar for designing the book cover and bearing with me. To Dottie De-Hart, I say thank you very much for listening to me for two years and believing I was going to publish *Journey*. Dottie is my publicist and she and her team helped to make my dream of publishing my book a reality. Dottie is also one of the most honest, *real* people I have met on the path to publishing, and for that I am extremely grateful and appreciative.

I am most appreciative of the source within me (within all of us), because my connection to the source (which I call God) is why *Journey* was written. I wrote only when I felt connected to the source, which made it easy, fun, and done in six months' time. *The source is always with us.*

Introduction

I didn't intend to tell my story. On September 19, 2006 at 4:30 a.m., I awoke from a dream in which I revisited a fear of mine from years ago.

I used to have a recurring nightmare. In the nightmare, I was trapped in a concrete maze on top of a building. I ran frantically through the maze, gasping for breath, looking for a way out. Every time I thought I was almost out of the maze, I turned a corner, only to run into a man much larger than me, dressed in black and wearing a white mask. I never knew who he was.

I haven't had this nightmare in years, and on that cool September night I wasn't actually having it either. I was dreaming about *remembering* the nightmare, looking at a cover for this book. I was noticing the book cover had exactly the same maze as the one in my nightmare.

What a transformation! I am amazed! What was once a symbol for my deep seated fear has become a symbol of what I am now going to share with you: the path and the journey out of fear and into love.

I chose the maze because I thought it would make a cool cover for this book. I did not make the connection between my choice for the book cover and the maze until I had the dream.

In my dream, after discovering the book cover featured the maze, I kept saying to myself over and over, *"I have to tell my story! I have to tell my story!"*

As I was dreaming, I didn't seem to feel thrilled about the realization of having to tell my story. I knew, though, that this story needed to be told.

Awakening from the dream, I replayed "my story" in my head so that I could tell it. I haven't told it in a long time. When I counsel people, I encourage them to tell their story once and move on as quickly as possible. *I want people to be present in the moment. I also want each of us to realize we have control over our lives in the present time, even if at one time in our lives, we may have had no control.* ***The focus is on becoming empowered.***

Here goes, here's my story. I think the best way to share my story with you is to tell it chronologically.

When I was 19 years old, I was in college and in a lot of pain. I couldn't sit still in my classes, I couldn't walk straight, and I didn't sleep well. The constant pain was ruthless.

I silently convinced myself that I must have some kind of terminal illness. I felt like I was dying. Finally, I went to see a chiropractor, who used kinesiology and gentle adjusting. He took x-rays and told me that I had the back of a 50 year old woman. I replied with conviction, "Try 100 years old!"

He went on to tell me that if I were to have children, I would have to have C-sections, because my hips and pelvic area were so twisted. Now I knew how messed up I was. *Lucky me,* I thought to myself.

After a lot of work between 19 and 21, and a regular routine of therapy, the doc did help me and I finally started to feel better.

When I was 21, I moved to Arizona, seeking a chiropractor who used kinesiology, and I found someone who used a technique called B.E.S.T. (Bio Energetic Synchronization Technique).

Using the B.E.S.T. technique, I felt better and better. Now, at 21, I began working out five or six days a week, something that I was not able to do when I was 19.

I fell in love, got married, and at 24, I became pregnant with my first child, and gave birth to Samantha at 25, without a C-section.

Two years later, I became sick with chronic sinus problems, which often turned into infections. I finally got sick and tired of being sick and tired and revisited my B.E.S.T. doctor, whom I saw whenever I felt the need.

On this particular sunny Arizona day, I felt as if I had surrendered. I entered the doctor's office waving my imaginary white flag. I was ready to be well once and for all.

The doc spoke two frightening words and a time frame. I was blown away! I had never shared my trauma with him.

The words were *sexual abuse.* The time frame was my childhood between the ages of one and five.

"Holy moley, Batman!" How did he do that? I was sexually abused just two months shy of my third birthday by a 16 year old neighbor. I now understood why the man in my nightmare was dressed in dark clothes and was so much taller than me.

The teenager who abused me was much darker in skin color than me. I was just a skinny little girl, with short blonde hair, wearing my yellow dress, not even three. I was oblivious to any kind of danger, because I was playing three houses down (as I often did) with my friends in the front yard.

The predator chose a concrete hall way entrance to his basement to abuse me. I was so small, so helpless. The concrete walls towered over me, without possibility of escape—*just like the concrete maze*!

The back of the house was shaded by a large tree. On that late April afternoon, the sun was in front of the house. The basement hall way was dark, damp and musty. The maze in my nightmare finally made sense.

The effects of the abuse were to surface again, however, in a very unsettling manner.

I have always loved and enjoyed watching my daughter. At the time she was two years old, however, watching her, so close to the age I was when I was abused, caused my body to remember and reconnect with my own experience at her age. I understood all my pain, which started at such a young age. Finally!

Wow! What a concept. My daughter was two and the memories of the abuse I experienced were showing up in my body as illness.

A quick look back at my childhood shed a little light on my physical state. I remember always being uncomfortable! Starting at about the age of 10, I used to walk my friends off the sidewalk. I simply couldn't walk straight.

Now, at 27, I found myself working together with the doc on that miraculous day, in his modestly decorated office. When the abuse came up, I was moved to a private room. The smell of vinyl and fresh paper as it crinkled under my face filled my senses. We cleared out the emotional interference.

One interesting note about my recurring sinus infections and recurring dreams: Before the year my daughter was two, I had never had a sinus infection. During the year my daughter was two, I had one sinus infection after another. Since that day 15 years ago, after clearing the emotional interference with the doc, I have never had another sinus infection.

Another amazing thing: Since that day, my recurring nightmare has never occurred again. What a relief! My life has never been the same, and we are talking in a *good way!*

Following the emotional and physical healing, I moved forward very quickly into the middle of the maze, well on my way to love.

Let's fast forward a bit, so I can share my life with you as I live it today. I am now 42. I feel better than I did at 19. I have four children. Contrary to the original prognosis instructing me to have C-sections, I was able to bring three of my children into this world with natural childbirth. (I opted for a C-section with one of my children because the baby's breech position posed a serious risk.)

I work out six days a week. I now hold a master's degree (by the age of 28, I was able to sit still and return to college). When I walk down the street with my friends, I actually walk in the direction I intend, and no one ends up off the sidewalk.

It is so good to be in charge of my life. Sometimes life can be a little scary because I don't always like what I create, but being in charge is so empowering! I have the power to recreate. I am in the driver's seat, I am empowered and life is great!

FEAR

Chapter 1
How Did I Get Here, Anyway?

Franklin Roosevelt was very wise when he said ***"The only thing we have to fear is fear itself."***

The introduction of this book tells you how I journeyed into fear. People end up in fear, and feel powerless over fear, in a multitude of ways.

Fear begins, for most of us, the moment we are born. Usually, all is well inside Mom's womb. If not, fear may actually begin at conception.

My point: Nearly everyone ends up living in fear at some time in their life. The exceptions are spiritual leaders such as Jesus, Buddha and Gandhi. If you could ask each of these spiritual leaders whether or not they experienced fear, what would they say?

Jesus, Buddha or Gandhi might respond by explaining that even they experienced fear, but knew how to shift quickly from fear to love.

With most of us, our fear begins with caregivers, such as parents, who are living in fear. We pick up their vibe. Children, however, are pretty good at not absorbing the fears of others, especially when they are younger than six.

Children are typically still close enough to the love they were in before they came here, and are joyfully oblivious to fear. *Children are more in the light than in the dark.*

For the most part, if you are living in an environment full of fear, you will probably pick up some of the fear. Then the ride begins!

Fear comes in all forms. *Anything other than love is fear at some level.* Fear ranges from very little to total fear.

Let's start the list of the many fears that haunt us. Fear of not having enough. Not enough money, love, success, or health. If you are raised by parents or guardians who have a fear that there is never enough money, you may start to notice as you get older (teenage years perhaps) that you are always counting your pennies and complaining that you don't have enough money, clothes, hair products, STUFF.

You are now headed down the same road as your parents or guardians. Fear of lack of money has been demonstrated to you, and you have well learned to believe the same, fearing lack of money.

Fantastic news! When you figure out that many fears are learned, you are in the perfect position to change directions. You don't have to take the same journey that your parents did.

Sincc I am a parent, I won't place all the blame on parents. You might possibly have picked up fear from any significant relationship you had growing up: a teacher, peer, minister, pastor or siblings.

I would like to share an example from my childhood. When I was about nine, my older brother told me that I couldn't do fractions. Since I thought he knew more than me, I believed him.

I went into fear about math, and I still struggle with fractions. (I don't care enough to choose a different path regarding this particular subject—that's a whole other story.)

I didn't do well in math until I went to college, when I decided for myself what I could and couldn't do. (A teacher can have the same effect by informing you that you aren't good at a particular subject. You believe this information to be the truth, because the teacher is the teacher.)

Let's return to the present. *We each have a past that creates our beliefs, and our beliefs create how we perceive things to be.* Good news! You are not a child anymore. You can take control of your own life! It is time to let everyone off the hook, including Mom and Dad.

Some children follow the beat of their own drum. These children do not believe anyone except themselves. More and more enlightened children are born every day. Listening to their own guts, children already know what we have forgotten about ourselves, and will soon remember.

Unfortunately, a lot of these powerful children are being labeled as either ADD or ADHD in an attempt (in my opinion) to shut them down. Check out my own son's experience.

When my son, Alexander was in fourth grade, his teacher insisted that he had ADHD, but I knew better.

With my background in social work, I spoke her language. I explained to her that since he did not display the symptoms of ADHD, I would not have him diagnosed.

We don't diagnose in my home. My belief in not labeling and diagnosing is why I chose not to continue in counseling as a profession.

Alex's teacher wanted him to be still in her classroom (good luck with a class full of nine year olds). My son was social, not ADHD. When Alex came home from school, he could easily sit still working on his homework and reading for two hours straight—and still does today!

My point: Do you have a child who doesn't believe everything the teacher says, or do everything the way the teacher wants? If so, you too may have a teacher wanting to label your child, in order to make life easier for the teacher.

Back to the present message. Of course, I am not describing all teachers, just the ones who don't know what to do with these powerful children. My answer to these teachers is "Run, now!", because there are more children like Alexander on the way.

Television creates a really quick trip on the avenue to fear. Turn on the news and listen to all of the uplifting stories. Wait -- there are none, or very few.

Most of the news is all about scaring the crap out of you. Television news perspective: If the news doesn't scare you or cause concern or worry, or better yet shock you, would you watch?

News reporters are just trying to keep their jobs. Sadly, when news reports scary stories, much of the public becomes frightened. We all become afraid that the subject of the story will happen to us.

For example: Some years ago, news reporters predicted the flu will be the worst on record. No surprise -- a huge number of people reported experiencing the exact symptoms described by the news story in vivid detail. Follow up story—we had one of the worst flu seasons ever.

Big surprise, right? I view this as the result of the old idea "You reap what you sow", "What you put out you get back", or more recently, *The Law of Attraction.*

The first time I ever heard about *The Law of Attraction* was several years ago at a B.E.S.T. seminar, conducted by Dr. M. Ted Morter, Jr.. He used *The Law of Attraction* to describe how people are like magnets. We put a thought out into the universe, and we attract to us the vibration of that thought.

If we think that we are vulnerable to the flu, because someone says we are, we can't stop thinking about it. Likely we will get the flu or at least sick. *Like attracts like.*

Instead let us think, "I am healthy and well" and really **feel** healthy and well. Even though others are sick, you will remain healthy and well.

Sounds too simple to be true, but it is. You see, part of the way that you also go into fear is by complicating things. As Albert Einstein once said, *"Any intelligent fool can make things bigger, more complex, and more violent. It takes a touch of genius -- and a lot of courage -- to move in the opposite direction."*

It really is quite simple. *Your beliefs become your reality, and your thoughts are all about what you believe.* Just change your mind about your beliefs and then your thoughts will change. "I am vulnerable to the flu", versus "I am healthy and well". Which belief attracts wellness?

"The significant problems we face cannot be solved with the same level of thinking we were at when we created them." Albert Einstein said.

In my opinion**, the only solution to solving your problems is to change your mind.**

News reports scare the general public about all kinds of things--not just health but also safety, getting ripped off, war, money, etc. Again, news people are just doing their job.

I suggest to anyone who owns a TV to watch any commercial. Commercials are also focused on fear. It seems that there are a lot of commercials featuring a drug you probably need for some symptom that you probably have.

Commercials compel you to take drugs to prevent what you don't have, but will be sure to get if you don't take the drug. Or, take the drug to cover up what you already have (probably because you didn't take the other drug to prevent yourself from getting what you got). Got it?

It's all so confusing isn't it? Like Dr. M.T. Morter, Jr. says in his book, <u>*The Soul Purpose, Unlocking the Secret to Health, Happiness, and Success,*</u> *"Medication addresses symptoms, not causes, and no pain or disease is caused by lack of medication."*

(It must have been the lack of Midol that caused me to be moody while I was on my period, or was it the lack of Tylenol that gave me my headache?)

In my opinion, I am sure that most drug companies don't promote discovering the cause of disease or illness.

Prevention methods put you in fear of catching or getting something. Cover up methods keep you from ever figuring out why you have what ever it is you already have.

You know what would be great? What if we could have a blocker on our televisions, similar to the pop up blocker on our computers?

The TV pop up blocker could block commercials designed to scare us into buying the advertisers' product.

I have another great idea --- a good news channel. We have the right to have a say about what we allow into our homes through the media. After all, we lock our doors to other intrusions we don't want in our homes.

I guess we do have the option to turn the TV off, or use something like a digital video recorder. We just can't control what is being shown to us on TV while we are watching unless you take one of two steps: 1) turn the TV off; or 2) use a digital video recorder.

Here is the challenge: *we still need to be able to live in this world just the way it is, and still be uplifted despite everything outside of us.*

How is this possible? Let us continue and see.

Your next question might be: shouldn't I be informed? If I'm not, doesn't that make me ignorant (or even worse) a bad citizen because I'm not informed?

My answer: You should only do what makes you feel good. If watching the news feels good to you, then fine.

What you really want to be able to do is to watch the news without having it affect you in a negative way. Most people, however, are affected by the news they watch.

If you're not such an enlightened person that the news doesn't bother you, then avoid it, at least until you are feeling pretty good from the inside out.

I have been studying and practicing uplifting, empowering information for over 20 years. I watch the news very rarely, and usually, only part of it. I personally do not enjoy the news, and most often, simply choose to watch something else.

My relatives accuse me of being uninformed, not concerned and unrealistic. I am very happy to live in my *own* very real world. I like the fact that I can choose what to include in my reality and what to leave out. This choosing is very empowering.

As for the relatives and others over the years who have accused me of being unrealistic, uninformed and unconcerned: When I look at them, and I look at me, I see very different people.

One is much happier—that's me. The same people who are pointing their fingers at me are some of the most miserable people I know—a fact reflected in every part of their lives.

It seems to me that their attitudes are negative, their careers are unhappy, they never have enough money and their personal lives are usually turbulent or almost non-existent.

Is this such a surprise? How much fun do you think you would have hanging out with people who think the news should be a major part of *your* life?

Okay, I'm being a little sarcastic. I'm sure that you can think of some people like this who you know too. Pay attention to those around you who aren't so happy and do a survey.

No big surprise with the results: Anxious people may be avid news watchers, readers and listeners. These unhappy people demonstrate an important lesson: How to get miserable fast, *or not*, partially by with what and whom you choose to surround yourself.

What other people think doesn't really matter. It's your life. How you feel is all that really matters.

Everyone takes their own individual journey. If it's your journey, why not make it joyful and fun? If you are able to watch the news and be okay, great. If you can't watch the news right now, you will be able to as you get healthier.

Can't wait right? Until then, don't worry. You won't miss anything. Just turn on your computer, go to work, or talk to a neighbor.

Some how, some way, the big news will get to you. I offer another example from a day none of us can forget. We each remember exactly where we were when we learned of the tragic events of 9/11.

I encourage you to intentionally surround yourself with good news as often as possible. When you hear bad news, you will have a much easier time dealing with the negativity than people who surround themselves with bad news most of the time.

Think of this as wearing extra padding for the big game. The big bad news won't take you down as easily as someone who has no good news stored in their memory.

View the bad news as what it is. Bad news won't feel good, but you'll immediately start moving toward the best possible perspective. Alternatively, the "finger pointer" will go down hard and say things like "I told you this world sucks."

You'll look for hope, while bad news people feel triumphant for the moment: The disaster validates everything they keep telling you. I'd rather look for hope. How about you?

We're not quite done exploring ways in which you move into fear. In fact, I could probably write the whole book on just this subject alone. Frankly, it would become boring. I'll just move through some of the ways in which we acquire fears. We can then start exploring those short cuts in the maze from fear to love.

By the end of this book, the maze walls will be both transparent and permeable, and your path will be clear!

I offer you another avenue towards fear to consider: *Buy in to what someone else tells you, and accept their statements as fact.* Your acceptance is usually because you have great respect for the source, or you are afraid not to believe them because you think they know more than you do.

Let's say you go to the doctor. He gives you a diagnosis of arthritis in your knees. He has only looked at you once, and asked you a couple of questions. You go home, and amazingly the pain becomes increasingly worse. You are then sent to a specialist to confirm the bad news you've already been given. Isn't that comforting?

Now there is no hope because you have been given the diagnosis by not one, but two doctors. You settle into the diagnosis, and the journey of arthritis begins. You think about the arthritis all the time, because *it* consumes your life. Everything you do has to take *arthritis* into consideration.

The changes you make to deal with the arthritis diagnosis keep arthritis in your face all the time. *It's* always there. You can't run, you can't hide, because *it* won't go away. Now you're stuck with *it.* Or are you?

A toxic "diagnosis" doesn't have to come from a doctor. The diagnosis can come from psychics, card readers, astrologists or even someone in the natural healing field.

The point: If you believe devastating news, you place your attention on the negative, and the negative is exactly what you will receive.

Remember *The Law of Attraction*? We are like powerful magnets. What energies we put out, we attract right back to us. *Like attracts like.* The doctor, astrologist, or healer is only telling you what they know.

What *you* can do is figure out what *you* know about *your* own well being. By the time you are finished reading this book, charting your own course will be easier for you.

You've probably heard the old saying "no pain no gain". A lot of people truly believe this, and live by this mantra. Typically, this message was conveyed to them as children, by parents, a coach, or older sibling. The message: Struggle is good and will make you a better person.

I guess it is supposed to be honorable to suffer. I think I remember getting this message as a child.

When you're having a hard time dealing with a boyfriend or girlfriend breaking up with you, you're told that in time (after you suffer a while) you'll be better off because you went through the suffering.

Who the heck wants to hear that? Why not look immediately and seek the good or positive in the break up, so that you can move on as quickly as possible?

Everyone may have to go through a similar experience in their own time. Why should you be set up to suffer for a long period of time? Your hurt may heal quickly, if you do not accept the "no pain, no gain" line of crap.

Even personal trainers, in recent years, have figured out "no pain, no gain" is false. You will likely injure yourself if you continue to work out while in pain.

Trainers tell you to be kind to yourself. Either take a break, or lighten up to give your body a break.

Lighten up, and give yourself a break by looking at the good in every situation as quickly as possible. The healing can then be *less painful with a whole lot gained.*

Sometimes we get so comfortable in our misery (because it is familiar) that we are always in fear. It just seems natural to feel the way we feel. No one has shown us a different way.

Misery has often been role modeled for us. Perhaps we learned a long time ago that we receive lots of pay offs for being unhappy or miserable.

Misery works for us. Those close to us unknowingly become our enablers. Our enablers mean well, but have fallen into our trap. We are not necessarily *consciously* aware that we have even set a trap.

The misery experience goes something like this: I feel unhappy and down. You come to my rescue and do something to help me feel better. You might buy me something, take me out, or just listen to me whine. The most important thing is that you join me in my misery. Please don't try to be the positive up lifter. That will just blow the whole thing for me, and I'll have to find someone else to fill the enabler role.

In fact, you would be better off if you just handed me a butt load of cash and left. Currency of any kind seems to be the answer for a lot of us, even if money is only a temporary fix.

Let's give some thought to drama. Drama is something that you have learned to create on a regular basis. Drama has become almost a life force for you. Again, drama has become comfortable because it is familiar.

If you have had a lot of drama in your life, the energy of drama becomes almost like oxygen. You have to have drama to survive. Drama gets you moving. Drama is an adrenalin rush.

I guess you could compare drama to being addicted to coffee. You look forward to that next cup because it makes you feel alive and energized.

If you are the enabler who gets sucked in by "the miserable one", then you too are in fear because you're taking on their stuff as your own. I know you're just trying to be the good friend who is loyal, sweet and nice. Give it up!

Being an enabler is only making you as miserable as the miserable person you are trying to rescue. Perhaps you might even become more miserable, because you can't change anything for the miserable one.

You've probably given Mr. or Ms. Miserable sound advice. Mr. or Ms. Miserable never listens to you, but you keep going back for more.

You are okay. It is good to be a good friend, but there is a better way. Be there for your friend as the positive up lifter who you are. Don't join them in their misery, because joining them will only perpetuate the situation.

Your miserable friend might even try to have a contest with you over who has the worst out of two miserable situations.

The contest could be something as silly as "my sore toe is worse than your sore toe". If your miserable friend doesn't want to hear your positive point of view, believe me, he or she will let you know.

Suddenly, he or she will remember to pick their dog up from the groomer or quickly have to leave for an appointment. Any excuse will pop up!

Mr. or Ms. Misery may decide not to remain friends with you because you won't play the misery game. Don't despair. You are probably both better off.

You will unload baggage that wasn't the right weight and size to take with you as you journey to love. The miserable ones may find their own map with directions to love, because they run out of other places to go.

You certainly don't have to end your friendship. Just don't sacrifice yourself for it. Be true to yourself and remain your own positive burst of joy, hoping others will follow your example.

If these friends stick around, they will probably start asking how or what you do to have such a wonderful life. That's when the fun will really begin in this co-created friendship.

When things seem to have gone badly for you, for as long as you can remember, you then expect things to go badly. Actually, if things do not go well, even for a short while, you may start to expect things to continue to get worse.

For example, if you believe bad things happen in threes, after number one you are waiting in expectation for numbers two and three. You may sometimes feel like you are stuck in a rut because you are having a hard time at work. You might begin to expect work to go badly on a regular basis.

"It just figures." "I'm not surprised." "That's my life." "Things never turn out for me." Such phrases become your mantra.

You are doomed. You start to wear a hood, (termed the *victim-hood).* A dark cloud follows you everywhere you go. Your attitude becomes like Eeyore's from Winnie the Pooh: *"Oh, Pooh…"*

Everything in your life begins to resemble pooh or poo, from your perspective. After a while, the load gets heavier and really starts to reek.

Being the victim you are, you begin to tell your story on a regular basis. You know, the one that goes something like, "My Mom was an alcoholic." "I was abused as a child." "My Dad never told me I was pretty." "I'm just not smart enough."

None of this stuff relates to *the now,* yet you continue with the attitude that "the world just isn't fair". You may often place yourself in a category, such as uneducated, plain, untalented, unworthy, broke, unhealthy, and ultimately powerless.

The doom and gloom you bring along everywhere you go can be a bit overwhelming, especially for people who are tuned in to positive, joyful energy. They may consider you a "drag".

If you expect things to go badly, then no surprise: Things go badly. The *Law of Attraction* is always working. What you think about is attracted to you.

Always remember, you are a magnet. *What you think about, you bring about.* Start to expect good things, even fantastic things, to happen, and watch you world change. See your morning going well, imagine it step by step, feel it, and then see what happens.

I'll share an experience from my life in which I got stuck in a rut about my hair. I kept having bad hair days, and started to dwell on bad hair. Amazingly, I had several bad hair days in a row.

Finally, the light bulb went on. I decided to change my thoughts. I said to myself, "I'm going to have a great hair day."

Guess what? I started having great hair days. My hair always looks okay, but when I consciously decide it's going to look great, what a difference!

I know hair isn't a big of a deal compared to other things, but it is a good place to start. Share my experience and turn things around.

If you start out having a bad morning, for example, you can stop and decide everything will get better. From the very moment you declare and affirm everything is getting better, you move toward being excellent. Think of the experience as kind of like making a wrong turn. You don't continue in the wrong direction, thinking about how horrible you feel about getting further and further away from your destination.

Instead, you just turn around and head in the right direction. *You are empowered when you realize that you can change the way things are going almost instantaneously.* Change really does happen in an instant.

The key is where you place your focus. If you have a bad thought, immediately think of something for which you are grateful. *Your attitude of gratitude cancels out the bad thought.*

I often use the birth of my children to think about, replacing bad thoughts with joyous ones. Sometimes just the thought of a pet results in your switching gears immediately. It is hard to feel bad while thinking about something that makes you smile, and therefore feel good.

I think that we have covered several ways in which you move into fear. I'm guessing you have come up with a few ideas of your own. We could go on and on, because there are all kinds of ways to get to fear.

I define fear as everything that doesn't fall into the category of *Love.* Dwelling on how you got in to fear will never get you through the maze, and on to the best possible place -- *Love.*

We can have fun, and even be funny, talking about how we get to fear.

We can have infinitely more fun hanging out together at the end of the maze, where *Love* lives. How wonderful life will be once you move into living in love. Nothing will ever be the same. Once you are living in *Love*, you will never want to go back to fear.

Chapter 2
Where Do I Go From Here?

By now, you have probably thought of several ways in which you have invited fear into your life. Don't beat yourself up over your invitation to fear. Everything is okay. You can change everything very quickly.

If you look at your life experience all at once, you will be overwhelmed. If you focus on the details of how you got into fear, you will never get out of fear.

Take note, and feel proud of your awareness of how fear has become a part of your life. The first step in getting healthier is awareness. However, dwelling on fear just keeps the yucky stuff alive. How has your life been affected by fear? Is fear sucking the life out of you? Are you now exhausted? Have you made yourself a priority, or has fear taken over?

You have to be okay with where you have been, and with where you are now, in order to move on to where you want to be. Stop telling your story! See only the good in where you are, and you will move quickly to where you want to be.

Eckhart Tolle, author of The *Power of Now*, writes, *"When you live your life in complete acceptance of what is, that is the end of all the drama in your life."*

I know a lot of you aren't sure how you will survive without your story, because your story has become such a big part of who you are. "I am the one whose father abused me," or "I am the one who was teased as a child." Now is the time to stop hiding behind your story. Stop using it as justification or validation for who you are and where you are.

I'm telling you! Your story has been dragged around for so long, it reeks like an old bag of poop. Throw it out. (Of course, you need to dispose of it properly. I'll talk more about proper disposal of old poop later.)

We cover up fear with busy-ness, weight, clutter, medication, drinking or even sleeping (probably a sign of depression). If you don't really love yourself then you are in fear. You are number one. How you treat yourself will teach others how to treat you also.

Where is your focus or attention? Is it on fear, or where you want to be?

I love this old Indian story. One evening an old Cherokee told his grandson about a battle which rages inside each person.

He said, *"My son, the battle is between two "wolves" inside us all. One is Fear. Fear is anger, envy, jealousy, sorrow, regret, greed, arrogance, self-pity, guilt, resentment, inferiority, lies, false pride, superiority, and ego.*

The other is Love. Love is joy, peace, love, hope, serenity, humility, kindness, benevolence, empathy, generosity, truth, compassion and faith."

The grandson thought about the story for a minute, and then asked his grandfather, "Which wolf wins?"

The old Cherokee simply replied, "The one you feed."

You might want to ask yourself, "Which wolf wins?" Right here, right now, in this very moment, you have the choice. Which wolf are *you* going to feed?

"I know of no more encouraging fact than the unquestionable ability of man to elevate his life by conscious behavior." wrote Henry David Thoreau.

From this point forward, begin to use your ability to elevate your life by conscious behavior.

Most of you have forgotten who you really are. You are probably thinking that *you alone* can't elevate your life. I guess now is a good time to remind you of who you are.

First, you must understand that the following is absolutely true. No one and nothing can turn the truth of who you are into falsehood, including your mother, father, brother, sister, spouse, teacher, minister, boss, yourself, or your debt, wrecked car, messy house, unruly children, lousy paycheck, bad teeth, bad haircut, gray hair, etc..

Whether you want to believe the truth or not is your choice.

The truth is (and always has been) that you are perfect, beautiful, powerful, valued, unconditionally loved and worthy, just to name a few of your innate gifts.

Look at a baby. You'll see that each baby begins life knowing this truth. We all came to this planet with all of the positive gifts named above.

Somewhere along the way we become mixed up, and forget who we really are. As I shared earlier, our confusion often occurs because we believe what someone else says about us is true. People who don't buy into what anyone else says get labeled as "trouble makers", "odd", "loners", or "ADHD".

These gifted people are right in remembering who they are. Those who live in fear are afraid of people who remember who they are, and in consequence, place negative labels.

If you don't follow the crowd, but instead follow the beat of your own drum, our society usually terms you as not normal. **I strongly suggest that you remember who you are and become incredibly *abnormal*.**

In turn, you are elevated to a point of pure love, peace, joy, and elation as often as possible.

Common *mediocrity attacks excellence.* People who are not at a higher level attack someone who is.

As Albert Einstein said, *"Great spirits have often encountered violent opposition from weak minds."* People living in fear feel uncomfortable in the presence of someone who is in an uplifted state, because **people living in fear are not** there, and can not comprehend the elevated consciousness.

If you follow the advice of Jesus, then you will *"Forgive them for they know not what they do."* It is natural that someone becomes defensive as a response to ignorance. Don't take it personally. People in fear are only responding from the level in which they are living. In fact, their response has nothing to do with you, and everything to do with them.

I know how hard it is to be patient with people who still haven't figured out that they have control over their own lives.

You may still be working on this yourself. Perhaps your own work may be part of why you are reading this book.

If you are already at a higher level, try to understand the reason that others who aren't there yet can't understand you. To them, you are speaking another language.

Another way of viewing your relationship to others: Consider yourself tuned in to a radio station which is out of their range. People in fear can't receive the information that you are receiving. From an energetic point of view, people in fear are vibrating at a lower frequency than you.

Remember: We are like powerful magnets attracting like things to ourselves. *Like attracts like.* For this reason, you are where you are, and others are where they are.

How do you use your unquestionable abilities to elevate your life by conscious behavior? *"I **believe** in living a poetic life, an art-full life. **Everything** we do is part of a **large canvas** we are **creating**,"* Maya Angelou wrote.

Look at your canvas. Clean off what you don't like or wipe the whole thing clean. Better yet, get a new canvas and get ready to start creating what you really want. You now are beginning to understand that you can in fact create your heart's desire.

Okay, I am getting excited for you, and I'm getting ahead of things. Let's just start with cleaning up the canvas. We'll see where we go from there.

You might want to keep some of what you have already created.

I think the best place to start is how you feel about yourself. We'll start with the inside, and work towards the outside. When you feel better inside, everything in your life looks better.

Your gray hair makes you look sexy and smart. Your old furniture is in vogue, and your unruly child is a unique, independent, and a free spirited soul.

I'm offering some simple examples so you can see how things will start to change. You'll start to see the good in everything. Then, and only then, the things that used to bother you in your personal life will start to change. All you have to do is change your focus.

You are powerful. The best part is that *you don't need to work hard or struggle to use your power to change your life.* No one even has to know what you're doing. People will simply respond to the new you.

You may receive a few strange looks at first, but feedback from those who really matter the most to you is likely to be positive.

Your nearest and dearest have probably been waiting for the *real* you to show up.

Do you like yourself? Look in the mirror and talk to yourself like a friend. Start affirming out loud what you like about the person in the mirror. It could be as simple as "You've got great teeth and a beautiful smile", "You have really pretty eyes", "You're a great listener", or "You're a great cook".

Just see how many gifts you can list. No one is listening so you can say whatever you want. Feel proud of the person in the mirror (yes, you!). Eventually you will recognize that you are proud of yourself.

I think that you will be surprised at how many things you like about yourself when you openly acknowledge your own gifts, with no one around to judge you. There will come a day when you will effortlessly recognize "How great thou art".

You might be wondering, who am I to rank myself up there with the *BIG GUY?* Marianne Williamson in *A Return to Love, (page 190) writes:*

"Our deepest fear is not that we are inadequate. Our deepest fear is that we are powerful beyond measure. It is our light, not our darkness, that most frightens us. We ask ourselves, "Who am I to be brilliant, gorgeous, talented, fabulous?" Actually, who are you ***not*** *to be?*

You are a child of God*. Your playing small doesn't serve the world. There is* ***nothing enlightened about shrinking*** *so that other people won't feel insecure around you. We are born to make manifest the glory of* ***God that is within us****. It's not just in some of us; it's in everyone. And as we let our own light shine, we unconsciously give other people permission to do the same. As we're liberated from our own* ***fear****, our presence automatically liberates others."*

I am writing this book for each person regardless of religious beliefs. If the word God bothers you, replace it with Source, higher power, higher self or whatever is most comfortable to you.

I do not believe that we are separate from our "Source". We are extremely powerful beings, especially when we remember to *connect* to our Source.

Colossians 3:11 says, "Christ is all, and in all." Yes, even though you aren't separate from "God", you can choose whether you are going to listen to "God" or not, just like you can choose whether to listen to anyone else.

You have free will. The difference is your "Source, God etc." is wiser than anyone else and knows your full potential.

Even if you believe that God is separate from you, you might also believe that you are a child of God. If this is true, you must know that God believes all of his children are powerful.

As He performed what we call miracles, Jesus said, "*And this too you will do and far more*". Often, God has more faith in you than you do in yourself. I believe that God expects *his children* to be great because greatness is the way He sees us.

I also believe we are all truly blessed. Many of us don't notice our blessings until a crisis arises, like a near death experience or chronic illness.

Don't wait for your world to come crashing down before you start counting your blessings. Start counting your blessings now. More than likely, your world may not come crashing down because "*Like attracts Like.*"

I've said it before, and I'll say it again. The *Law of Attraction* is the most powerful law in the universe. We'll address the *Law of Attraction* in more detail later.

The lights are going on all over the place for you now because you are becoming **aware or awake.**

- Aware and Awake equal clarity.
- Clarity equals power.
- Power equals movement.
- Movement equals change.
- *Life is movement and change.*

Life offers you the opportunity to become awake, clear, powerful and to move toward change. Life is so much fun and there is never a dull moment, *if you choose.*

Another wonderful fact about life; you get to **choose** how to live and what you include. Do you feel the power?

I think that now is a good time for you to listen to the song *"The World's Greatest"* by R. Kelly. Start dancing and celebrating your *Greatness.*

I have to tell you, if you aren't celebrating by now, I don't know how you are containing your joy in knowing how wonderful you are, and what a great opportunity life is. You are free to choose to take a fabulous journey and have fun the whole way.

Celebrating yourself everyday is essential to having the life that you want. Choose to treat yourself well. It might be easier for you to start treating yourself well by thinking of yourself as a friend or a child who is seeking guidance in how to start feeling better overall.

What would you tell your friend or a child who (just by chance) has the same exact life as you? My suggestion: Take your own advice, I bet it's great.

Usually, we feel more comfortable when we are standing outside a situation/circumstance. From the objective perspective, we see exactly what the answers are. When we have a situation in our own lives, it is harder to see what is right in front of us.

No, you don't need a counselor. Save your money. Remember, you have the power to change your own life. Why do we so often feel that we need to go to an outside source to figure out what to do next?

I think part of the reason is because we don't trust ourselves to know. As we considered previously, we have been told, in a variety of ways, that we simply don't know anything worth trusting. We received this message from parents, siblings, teachers and TV, just to name a few avenues we have traveled in order to believe this great lie.

If a friend complains to you that he or she is feeling run down and wiped out from a long day of work, what do you suggest? Since I can't hear your answer, I will tell you what I might say to a friend.

"Why don't you order your favorite Chinese food? While you are waiting, have a nice cup of your favorite tea. Order some food for your family as well. Take the night off from cooking. Get yourself ready for bed early. Perhaps you might enjoy a bubble bath, a good book or a favorite sitcom. Breathe in and out before you fall asleep. Review in your heart and mind all that you are grateful for in your life."

This is just the beginning. When you start to recognize that you are feeling out of sorts, take action on the advice you would offer a friend. *Learn to be your own best friend.*

When you get more comfortable, you will be able to talk straight to yourself with the kindness and care of a loving friend. *We need to be kind to ourselves first.*

Kindness will then flow over into all of our other relationships.

How you treat yourself is an indicator of how you feel about life overall. Everything starts with you. You have to become your own first priority.

Soon, you will be able to treat yourself well all of the time, not just when you are feeling out of sorts or wiped out. Feeling good is good for your health in general. As a bonus, feeling good feels good!

It is impossible to attract good things into your life if you are feeling bad. "What you put out is what you get back." I offer you a simple fact-- it's good to feel good. When you feel good, your life improves dramatically and often quickly.

Feeling bad is building a brick wall between you and the good things trying to enter your life. You block the good from coming to you.

In other words, life can't get good—the quality of your life can not improve -- if you are feeling bad. Hopefully, this factual information motivates you. I don't know about you, but I can never experience too much good in my life. Since it all starts with you, let's get back to how else you can prioritize yourself.

As you go through your day, start to notice if you are feeling good or not. For example, if you notice that you aren't feeling happy, look at what you are doing, and how you are feeling about it. Let's imagine a typical morning. You get up; get ready for your day, and your spouse looks at you. You snap, "What?" Stop. Take note. Are you perhaps a little cranky? Why?

Acknowledging your feelings is very healthy. You are not cranky because your spouse looked at you. Consider whether or not you are faced with something you don't want to do today.

At the moment in which you realize where your frustration is coming from, you can begin to turn things around. You might start by apologizing to your spouse for snapping. Share with your spouse, and explain that you are dreading the task you have ahead of you. Perhaps your spouse might even be able to offer you another way of looking at the source of your grumpiness, or perhaps not.

The most important thing is to see the good in what you have to do. The good aspect may be that after today, the unpleasant task will be done. Perhaps completing this task is the good, or this task will open the door for better things to come.

Really, it isn't so hard to find something good in almost any situation. The good doesn't have to be huge. All the good aspect has to do is give you a sense of relief, or point you in the direction of feeling just a little better.

You have probably heard the phrase "fake it until you make it". I am not suggesting that you fake it. If you already know that you are not being authentic with yourself, then faking it won't have a lasting affect anyway.

Realize what you are really grateful and thankful for, and don't fake it. There are lots of things for which to be grateful. Start with the obvious. You are breathing. You have a place to live. You are thankful for your children, your dog, or simply for the food you have to eat. Think of these seemingly simple things. *Feel* the gratitude you have for each.

Take a lesson from a dog or a young child. For example, spend some time observing a dog for a while.

For our canine friends, the whole purpose is to have fun and enjoy life. Dogs want to be outside, chase a ball, have a belly rub and slumber in the sun. Dogs indulge in lots of siestas. I think our canine friends are definitely on the right track.

Dogs also love to put their heads out the car window. People who own convertibles, on the other hand, rarely put the top down for fear of messing up hairdos.

Either way, we are living in fear, and the dog is living in love with life. Dogs appear to treasure every waking and sleeping moment.

Have you ever watched young children at play? The kids are all about having fun. There is no fear involved at all, unless a concerned (fearful) adult intervenes, and advises something to fear.

"Don't climb so high." "Slow down before you fall." "You're going to poke an eye out." Is it possible that the adult is speaking in a way attracting mishap or injury?

Instead, the adult could offer, "Have fun, be safe." I perceive a lot less fear in this statement. "Have fun, be safe", is more an affirmation that the children are already safe, than a statement implying fear of injury. The affirmation indicates a tone of confidence that the child *will* be safe. Safety and fun are the expectations.

As parents, we teach our children what to believe. Recently, my seven year old daughter Mariah drew a picture. She then exclaimed, "I'm really good at this!" I responded, "Yes, indeed, you are an artist!" Mariah's face lit up with pride and a big smile.

We are all artists in are lives. Remember Maya Angelou's thoughts: "**Everything** we do is a part of a **large canvas** we are **creating."** Children and dogs seem to understand what life is really all about. They are definitely living closer to love.

I think this is why older people respond so well to children and their canine buddies. Many (not all) people around age 70 and older reach a point in their lives at which they remember who they are.

We often observe people in their later years acting like children. If this perception is true, older people are heading back to where they came from -- a place of pure, positive peace, joy and love.

I think that older people who can't seem to get to this higher place of being may often experience memory problems, become unable to communicate any longer, or even die.

Since taking courses in college about deterioration which often occurs in later years, I have thought about why many older people "check out" either mentally or completely.

I think the "checking out" occurs because they can't handle being here anymore, or choose to not deal with being here anymore.

I am pretty sure that not being fully present in the here and now is an attempt to be in a (checked out) place feeling closer to love. Zoning out is kind of like being high. Sometimes, zoning out can feel a whole lot better than being present. Zoning out is a way of tuning out uncomfortable noise.

In my opinion, people who are "checked out" long ago bought into the notion of being only human, and have forgotten their greatness.

I also think that many other older people who are fully present have a great attitude about life and are very wise. Personally, I believe those who die earlier are wise as well. They may realize all is better after they die.

Be aware! Very aware! You don't have to die to live a fabulous life right here and now. *The Journey from Fear to Love* is about **living** the best life possible. You truly can live heaven on earth.

Having some quiet time everyday is very beneficial. I know it's hard to find the time. Having four children has made me very creative in finding the time for myself.

I set my alarm 15 minutes earlier than I need to. I lie in my bed, breathe in and out, and focus on the mantra I created over time.

I affirm and feel over and over, *"I am perfect, beautiful, and powerful. I am abundant and joyful, unconditionally loved, worthy and valued. My body is emotionally and physically balanced and aligned. I move with ease. Everything, everything always goes well for me."*

This mantra may seem a little long, but it works for me. You have to come up with what works for you. I enjoy my mantra before I go to bed, and before I get up in the morning. My mantra sets the tone for my day and my sleep.

Remembering how wonderful I am feels really good. I didn't start out with the current large list of my gifts. As time progressed, I realized that I had a lot of good things to say about who I am.

Start with whatever you come up with first. I have something to tell you that is certainly true for you and everyone else: ***"You are worthy."***

Affirm out loud: *I am worthy*! I have worked with a lot of clients over the years. The most frequent belief I find invading people's hearts is the sense of unworthiness.

I believe this belief of unworthiness alone is the root cause of most problems, physical or emotional.

It is impossible to have good things come to you if you are feeling bad. The law of attraction just doesn't work this way. Sometimes people say "I just had a car accident and I was feeling really good that day." The key to the mystery: He or she may have been feeling really good *that day*, but how was that person feeling for days, weeks, even months or years prior to the car accident?

The fact that the car accident occurred on a day when he was feeling good is perhaps why he may not have been hurt badly. All the people he needed to help him after the accident were available. The availability of the help he needed is not a coincidence.

I believe that if he had been in a more positive mode for a longer period of time, perhaps he might not have attracted the car accident at all.

Mother Teresa said, "*There is more hunger for love and appreciation in this world than for bread.*" The love and appreciation has to start with you. If you don't love and appreciate yourself, then you can't love and appreciate anyone else. *You* be the example.

Marianne Williamson writes, "*And as we let our own light shine, we unconsciously give other people permission to do the same. As we're liberated from our own* ***fear****, our presence automatically liberates others.*"

Don't tell me we aren't powerful. We are so powerful; we can make our lives miserable or wonderful just by choosing where we focus our attention. With laser like attention, you can pinpoint things that make you feel better, or things that make you feel worse. What you choose to zoom in on will become the primary tone of your life.

Once again, you might want to ask yourself which wolf you are feeding. If you choose to shine, not only will you feel better, but you will have a positive effect on anyone with whom you choose to come into contact, if even for only a moment.

I saw two bumper stickers recently. One said "Don't believe everything you think." The other said, "Change is inevitable, growth is optional." I don't know who came up with these, but the authors are very wise.

The advice "Don't believe everything you think" is excellent. If we stop every so often to notice what we are thinking, we could save ourselves a lot of heart ache.

It is very difficult to focus on every thought we have. An easier, more practical strategy: Notice and feel how you are feeling first. Next, figure out what you are thinking about that is causing your feelings.

Change your thoughts. If the thought is recognized as causing you to feel bad, and not good, discard the negative thought! Focus on a thought that makes you feel better.

Let's use the example from Chapter One. "I am vulnerable to the flu", versus "I am healthy and well". You choose the thought that makes you feel better. This process is not rocket science.

For many reasons, we believe that getting to a place of feeling good is difficult. Let's change this thought. Instead of "getting to a place of feeling good has to be difficult" how about, "feeling good is easy". Simply choose not to believe that "getting to a place of feeling good has to be difficult". Recall the bumper sticker "*Don't believe everything you think.*"

The second bumper sticker, "*Change is inevitable, growth is optional*", is also very true. If you are changing in healthy, positive ways, I believe that growth and expansion will naturally occur.

If you are bouncing around from one bad feeling to the next, growth and expansion cannot occur unless you decide to stop and see something good in all that is happening. Perhaps you can learn something from your situation or experience. Looking at everything that happens in your life as happening *for you, and not to you* is very important.

For example, I contracted with a chiropractor while I lived in Arizona. My job included marketing for him as well as assisting him in his office with patients.

I made a commitment to the chiropractor: I would have him and his practice featured on the local news. Within four months, I fulfilled this commitment. The news story lasted about four minutes.

Trailers were broadcast all day, leading up to the feature.

The four minute story was beautiful. I previously arranged a conference room in a local hotel, scheduled for two days following the broadcast. The chiropractor planned to speak about fibromyalgia.

I called the reporter the day of the story. I requested that the date, time and location of the chiropractor's talk be announced. She was wrapping up the story, and added the information about the talk at that very moment.

An audience of 200 attended. Originally, I was hoping for 30. What a night!

The following Monday morning, 79 patients were scheduled for appointments. Previously, the chiropractor had been seeing 25-35 patients a day. I felt triumphant.

As time moved forward, it became apparent that I appreciated and valued myself more than the chiropractor did. This is really the way it should be. As previously discussed, we should appreciate ourselves first and foremost. I was having a hard time working in a place where I wasn't valued and respected. It didn't *feel good,* so I gave my notice and left.

At first I was very angry at his lack of appreciation for me because his attitude caused me to leave. "Why would he do this *to me* anyhow?" I wanted to scream.

Soon I realized his behavior had nothing to do with me and everything to do with him. He obviously wasn't functioning as close to love as I was. I sent unconditional love his way.

The process took a while and a lot of forgiveness. Eventually I had to remind myself that *everything happens for you not to you*. What part of this experience happened *for me*?

I learned a lot working with this chiropractor. I learned how *not* to treat patients/clients, and people who are working with or for me. I learned that I could accomplish anything I decided to do.

I also learned to honor, respect and value myself. If that meant leaving a job, then I left the job.

Finally, I learned that I am strong and powerful. I don't need anyone else to tell me that I am strong or powerful. Wow! It did happen *for me.*

The idea that everything happens *for you and not to you* reminds me of a three and a half year relationship that I had with a man.

I thought I was going to marry him. I met Bob my senior year of high school. I was 17 and he was 21. He was a great guy, and lots of fun. He drank a little too much, but at 17 that didn't seem like a big deal to me. Bob went back to college and I started college as well. We attended the same university.

I thought he would change, and stop drinking before we got married. That's not what happened. I loved everything else about Bob but his drinking.

"Why wouldn't he care enough about me to give up drinking?" I said over and over to myself. Instead, he started drinking more, and became difficult to be with. He turned into not such a nice guy.

He told me he would smoke pot in our home, and in front of the children we planned to have someday. I recall that sadly, I was wearing his Grandmother's engagement ring. (Bob's parents had given him the engagement ring as well as the wedding band to give to me. The engagement ring was a large diamond ring and the wedding band featured several diamonds.) His family had some money, and they liked me very much. I think they hoped I would make Bob a better person.

By the time I was 20, and Bob was 24, I began to see that he wasn't going to change. I had also started treatment from the chiropractor who told me that I had the back of 50 year old woman.

I began to heal. As a result, I was getting healthier emotionally as well as physically. Since I wasn't in constant pain, I was able to focus more on my emotional health than before.

I still wanted the answer to the question: "Why is he doing this *to* me?", especially when our wedding day was only three months away. Since I couldn't come up with an answer that made any sense to me, I called the wedding off.

I knew that I didn't feel good in this relationship, and I deserved better treatment. After breaking up, I felt I had invested a lot in my relationship with Bob I asked myself, "What for?".

It was all *for me!* Isn't that a wonderfully delicious way to look at everything that happens in your life? Life is all good if you can see that it is all *for* you.

Back to our present. I get tingles every time I realize what the *for* is, even if it is something that has already happened. I am reminded of how I have arrived at the wonderful place where I am today.

If something happens in the present *for me*, I realize how grateful I am for the experience, which is always enlightening. Instead of saying the common phrase "What the f----?" (Although this may not be the language you speak out loud, we all relate to the emotion behind this phrase.)

Try to say, "What *the for*?" *For me* invites energies of having an enlightening experience, rather than having something happen *to you* again.

With regard to my relationship with Bob there was a lot that happened *for me*. I learned what I want and what I didn't want in a relationship. Marrying someone with a drinking problem is not something I ever want.

I'm grateful for my relationship with Bob. Without it, I might have discovered the hard way that I didn't want to be married to someone who liked to drink a lot.

Bob had many qualities I did want in a husband. He was intelligent, he was fun, and he was often very thoughtful. I realized my own power through our relationship, and called the wedding off.

You can't change someone else. You can choose not to be with or around unpleasant people. Whether others agree with your choice is not important. Your choice is okay.

When I broke up with Bob, several people, including his parents, tried to talk me out of my decision. Friends who tried to convince me to go through with the wedding later saw Bob drunk several times. They later apologized for giving me a hard time about my decision.

Can you see? **You are the only one who knows what is best for you.** I learned to trust myself. I learned to make good decisions for myself. I learned to rely on *what felt right to me.* My inner strength came forth and has remained as a part of who I am today.

In Chapter One, we explored several ways in which we get into fear in the first place. Chapter Two has given you some ideas about what to do, now that you have become aware of fear in your life.

Stop telling your story! Be okay with where you are and where you have been.

- *Uncover the cover ups* you may be using to disguise fear.
- *Love yourself like your best friend.*
- *Remember to never forget who you are.*

When you stop, uncover, love and remember, you will be able to follow the beat of your own drum and *become.* When you *become,* you will then *do* and *have* all that you so desire.

Become an artist, but first clean up your canvas. Let your own light shine, and remember how great thou art. Let dogs and children teach you.

Spend some quiet time everyday. Celebrate your life everyday. Acknowledge your feelings, and when you need to, change your thoughts.

Know that nothing happens *to you.* Everything only happens *for you.* Finally, bask in the growth and expansion which naturally follows.

Be patient and kind to yourself. Pat yourself on the back as you acknowledge the progress you are making. As you feel better, life will get better. Before long, life will be utterly fantastic!

Chapter 3
Go Within and Reconnect to Your Source

We have already considered Source can have different meanings for different people. Don't get caught up in semantics. Use whatever term for the Source that feels right to you.

I call Source God, Source or Higher Self. As we have already considered, children tend to be naturally connected to Source. Let me offer an example from my own youth. I remember when I was abused at the age of two, almost three. I was very frightened about telling anyone. The boy who abused me told me that he would kill me if I said a word to anyone.

I really didn't know exactly what he meant, but I knew that it was very bad. I also knew that if you "**killed**" an ant it stopped moving *forever.* I didn't tell anyone about the abuse for about three years. I still remained connected to Source.

The dark terrified me. This was probably partially normal for my age, but intensified due to the fact that I was abused in the dark.

Every night I had an experience that remains very vivid to me to this very day. I would close my eyes to go to sleep. Suddenly, I would be falling into a dark spiraling hole. Falling was a most joyous, exhilarating ride. As I was freefalling, I felt completely supported by someone or something.

Love surrounded and carried me. Fear was not a part of this experience at all. Just before falling a sleep, as I got to the end of the hole or tunnel, a bright light filled the space. When I fell back into the space, I was out like a light.

Especially interesting to me: as soon as the light came on, I fell asleep for the night. I realized years later that as a child, every night I connected to my Source/God. I fell back into the lap of God.

As a child, all I knew was that the experience felt good, so I was happy to go for the ride every night. When *Source* calls a child, the child is usually wise enough not to question the call, and simply follow.

Now, in the present, I'm talking about the natural way that children will listen to God. There are all kinds of stories about how children survive tragedy because they hear someone say for example, "play dead", or "don't walk that way, instead take the next street". The child is left unharmed because the child listened.

"There wasn't anyone there", is the report a child offers. The little one just listened, followed directions, and remained safe.

The first verse from Alabama's song, *Angels Among Us*, tells us:

I was walking home from school on a cold winter day.
Took a shortcut through the woods, and lost my way.
It was getting late, and I was scared and alone.
But then a kind old man took my hand and led me home.
Mama couldn't see him, but he was standing there.
And I knew in my heart, he was the answer to my prayers.

The singers offer us a couple of other lines in the song:

Oh I believe there are angels among us.
To guide us with a light of love.

The title of this song sounds like a lot of the stories shared by children who have been in perilous situations.

Back to my childhood. When I was six years old, I recovered from my fear of being killed like an ant. I started telling anyone who would listen about "what that boy did to me".

My recovery from the fear of being murdered is an example of how much closer to *Love* a child is than an adult. It didn't take me long to *get over my fear of being killed*, because I was still connected to my Source/God.

You can guess how close to love and how far from fear you are by how closely you are connected to Source/God, because *God is Love.*

It is impossible to be connected to God and experience fear simultaneously. I was definitely no where near fear because the first person that I told about the abuse was the boy's sister. She was my friend, and I told her as my friend. I wasn't trying to get him in trouble.

Apparently, after the abuse occurred, my Mother knew that he had attempted to do *something* to me. She didn't know the extent of the abuse until I was about six. Only then was I able to share more with her. I wasn't feeling well, and I said that it was because of what he had done to me.

When the boy's father heard that I still remembered, he felt terrible and moved his family. According to my parents, he didn't want me to have to be reminded of the abuse by the physical presence of his family.

Their absence probably helped me to be able to move on. Obviously, their moving away didn't make me forget the experience. I did, however, forgive this boy a long time ago. I also continue to feel appreciation toward the boy's parents for their compassion.

His parents were always very nice to me. Appreciation is another emotion which brings you closer to Love/Source.

On to my teenage years--I now remember and realize when I was a teenager my Source (God) was always trying to get my attention. Due to the abuse I experienced, my self esteem was in the toilet (my official diagnosis). I often felt inferior. If God was talking, I wasn't listening.

I think most people don't listen. We get wrapped up in our personal dramas, and we are so distracted that we can't hear God. If God were screaming at the highest possible volume, we still wouldn't hear because we are just too preoccupied and busy.

The feeling of being overwhelmed definitely takes us further from Source. It is not that we don't want to hear God/Source. We just can't hear over our own noise. We need to clean up our connection so that our signal is clear.

Quiet your mind through meditation, yoga, exercise or whatever works for you. Or, ***just breathe, for crying out loud!***

Seriously, breathing is something that we often forget to do. Just breathing deeply will wake you up and help you tune you into Source. Discouraged people might say "God isn't listening", and give up.

The fact is that it is *not* God Who needs to be listening to you. It **is you who needs to be tuned in, and *listening to God.*** *Your God or Source is your Higher Self. Therefore, God is always tuned into you.* If you aren't hearing God, Source, or higher self, you are energetically vibrating at a lower level. When you are vibrating or functioning at a higher frequency, you become more open to listening and receiving messages when Source is communicating with you.

How do you know if you're connected to Source or not? You need to ask "How do I feel?" I know that I was completely connected to God during my childhood when I experienced the free fall into the spiraling tunnel, ending in light. I felt pure love and joy.

Feelings of love and joy are pretty good indicators that you are connected to Source, which is closer to Love.

Feeling negative emotions is an indicator that you are disconnected from your Source, and closer to fear. Looking back to the time when I was a teenager and disconnected, I began to experience a lot of physical pain. I had pain in my hips, back and feet. The physical pain was also a sign of living more in fear than love. Another way to express the cause of my physical pain was my disconnection to God.

The process of (re)connecting to God is not rocket science, as I have indicated before. We all make things too complicated. We have been taught for the most part that we have to suffer to get to the good stuff.

Many churches preach the need to suffer. Suffering with compliance, according to these churches, will result in rewards sometime after you're dead.

I do believe automatically wonderful experiences await you after you're dead. For this present moment however, living is a cooperative effort. Source is always in cooperation with you.

All you have to do is feel good to get to the good stuff. Feeling good keeps you in cooperation with Source. God/Source wants to bring everything that is good for you into your reality.

With suffering comes more suffering. After you're dead, it doesn't matter whether you suffered or not while you were here. Either way, your experience will be great after death.

While you're here, why not be in joy as often as possible? You can choose to create heaven right here on earth. Your joy is all about being able to see the good in any situation.

About six years ago, my husband and I were having financial difficulties. My husband thought that the only solution was to declare bankruptcy.

I had no idea that we were having problems because at the time my husband was in charge of our finances. He made some decisions that put us into a financial hell. (He would not make those decisions again today.)

At first I was angry (disconnected) and became very ill for about eight weeks. Distraction equals not listening to the call of Source. For eight weeks, while Source was calling me, I tried to listen, but it was hard.

I did get myself out of bed everyday. I took a walk, came home and did my exercise routine. Then I did the smartest thing I could have ever done.

I sat on my swing, closed my eyes and went over everything in my head for which I was grateful and thankful. This attitude of gratitude helped to quiet my mind, so that I could hear over my own noise.

(Quieting your mind is very similar to meditation—neither is very easy at first.)

I started with the basics. I was grateful for having a home, food to eat, my children and my dogs. As time went on, the list became longer. I added my husband, my parents, my siblings and their families, my in-laws, nieces and nephews.

Then I started sending love out to everyone, including my neighbors, and especially to my husband. Notice I was so angry, my husband didn't make the first cut on my list of gratitude. He wasn't added until the second round. He might not have known this. I would like to send him a special message at this moment. *Honey I love you. All this is really water under the bridge. I am writing a book and you know I have a lot of integrity. The truth needs to be told.*

The point I am making is that I sent the most love to the one with whom I was the angriest. Why would I do that?

The reason is simple. The anger was keeping me disconnected from Source. At the time, I didn't have that awareness at a conscious level. I did know that I felt better when I sent love to my husband rather then anger.

Bingo! Connection completed. At this point, I received an answer to our financial problem. I was sitting in this grateful and thankful space. Like a lightening bolt out of nowhere, I realized that I could refinance my home.

Please recall that my home made the first cut on my gratitude list. I guess our home appreciated my gratitude, because our home saved our butts.

I called my friend Dan who worked in the loan department at a local bank and I asked him if he thought that I could refinance my home.

"Absolutely," he said. "The rates are at an all time low right now." With my husband in Ireland on business, I refinanced our home.

Another perk of connection to God/Source: since you are not in fear, you can do anything you set your mind to. If I were not connected to God/Source, I could not have accomplished the refinance.

My nature does not allow me to take such a big step without my husband by my side.

Here is the coolest part of this story. I needed to save $1100 per month in order to keep from declaring bankruptcy. When Dan called me back to let me know the refinancing had gone through, I asked him how much I was going to save per month.

Dan replied; now get this, $1100. Not $1000 or $1099. It was *exactly* $1100. Wow! I still get chills today when I think about the miraculous results.

Do you think I was listening to Source or not? When I listened to God/ Source, how do you think my attention to Source worked for me? Pretty gosh darn fantabulous, right?

With this example from my life, you can see how connection to Source/God works. When I started to see the good in my situation, and I felt gratitude in the middle of what felt devastating, the answers to resolve our current problem came and came fast. One answer solved a huge dilemma for my family.

If I had not *slowed down enough to connect to God,* I would never have come to any solution. Of this I am sure. My head would have continued to spin with the idea of devastation and devastation would have continued to follow. As I recognized and expressed gratitude, more and more flowed forth for which to be grateful and thankful.

While going through this process I also recognized that I was **accountable** for being exactly where I was. I couldn't blame my husband for my *own journey* to financial hell. I will discuss *accountability* more later.

I decided to feed the loving wolf. Remember: that which you think about and feel about, you bring about.

Hating or loving. Which are you doing most often? One will connect you to Source. Can you guess which one? The other will prevent you from being connected.

What is the result from hating your job, your neighbor, or even your clothes? You are not heading in the direction bringing you greater connection to God, which is Love. You are going the wrong way, and holding yourself back from your Source.

Complaining that others have more than you will not bring you closer to what you want. Complaining that others have more will, in fact, continue to block your Source connection.

Griping about the wrong that someone has done to you might feel like relief or release. If you are stuck in the space of griping and don't move into gratitude, you are disconnected.

You might be justified and correct about the wrong which has been done to you. So what? While you are expending energy in being self righteous and right, you are distancing yourself and cluttering your connection to God.

Would you rather be right and miserable? Would you rather be happy? Let it go! *My mother always told me that anger toward another is like giving yourself poison and expecting the other person to die. In reality you are the only one suffering. (Thanks,* Mom.*)*

It is to your great benefit to let go of toxic energy coming in the disguise of anger or resentment. By continuing to hold on to the anger instead of forgiving the person, you are abusing yourself. The message that you are sending to your Source is that you want to keep recreating exactly where you are.

Where are you? Stuck in the muck? "What the for?" is the question you should ask next in order to help yourself get out of the muck. Start moving toward the other end of the maze into love.

In order to move toward fuller connection to your God, Source or Higher Self, your goal should always be to seek thoughts which elevate you, perhaps of gratitude and love, and thoughts which make you feel better. Negative thoughts equal toxic discomfort. Positve, uplifting thoughts equal comfort, relief and feeling better overall.

The better you feel, the closer you are to Source. I know it is hard to always come up with a thought which feels better on the spur of the moment.

My suggestion to my clients is to find an anchoring thought. An anchoring thought is something that gives you warm fuzzies every time you think that thought. Some examples of anchoring thoughts might be the birth of your child, your wedding day, or holding your pet. It is up to you. Your anchoring thought should bring up a purely joyful feeling when you think about it. This anchoring thought then can be used as a quick tool to redirect you towards love, especially when you're in a tight spot.

Let's use work as an example. Lots of distractions lead you to feel negative emotions. Focus on your anchoring thought—even if only for a moment. You will return to a better feeling place. The anchoring thought results in a powerful positive response turning you in the right direction in an instant.

An anchoring thought is like carrying a magic bullet with you all of the time, wherever you are. Similar to carrying a gratitude stone or coin in your pocket, the anchoring thought just needs to be pulled out to remind you of all for which you are grateful.

According to Dr. Masaru Emoto, author of *The Hidden Messages in Water*, gratitude and love are the most powerful emotions. The combination of the two will wipe out any negative emotion in a heart beat.

"It is my firm belief that it is love that sustains the earth. There only is life where there is love. Life without love is death. Love is the reverse of the coin of which the obverse is Truth." (Mahatma Gandhi.)

Dr. Emoto's research with water demonstrates when water is exposed to different words, water forms different crystals. His research is more complex than my description. You'll have to read his book to gain more insight.

According to Dr. Emoto, *"The water shown the words love and gratitude forms the most beautiful crystals. Of course the word love alone has the ability to create wonderful crystals, but love and gratitude combine to give the crystals a unique depth and refinement, a diamond-like brilliance."*

Water exposed to negative words, such as hate, created incomplete, unattractive, even ugly crystals, according to Dr. Emoto's research.

Dr. Emoto also considers fetuses. We begin life as 99% water. When we our born, we are 90% water. As adults, we are 70% water. If we die of old age, we will be approximately 50% water. *Dr. Emoto observes, "In other words, throughout our lives we exist mostly as water."*

Draw your own conclusion. I think his research confirms the fact that our emotions affect our overall well-being. Water can be dramatically affected, just by exposure to words.

We are mostly water. Our overall health and well-being are dramatically affected by our emotions and feelings.

The more you are connected to your Source-- which is closer to love-- the more you will experience well being in all areas of your life.

"When you are living a full and enjoyable life, you feel better physically, and when your life is filled with struggles and sorrow, your body knows it. So when your emotions flow throughout your body, you feel a sense of joy and you move towards physical health. Moving, changing, flowing -- this is what life is all about." Dr. Emoto states.

The saying "go with the flow" takes on new meaning when you realize that *you are the flow*. The natural flow of well-being really does lie within you.

Recall our conversation about vibrating or functioning at different levels, and how those different levels affect how open you are to hearing Source. (Let us recall that children naturally vibrate at a higher level.)

Dr. Emoto states that *"Human beings vibrate 570 trillion times a second, a number that exceeds the imagination and indicates incredible and wonderful hidden potential."*

If you are vibrating at a higher level, meaning closer to Source or God, which is Love, then you are able to create an incredible life full of joy, exceptional happiness and well being.

I have to say it again: **we are incredibly powerful!** At 570 trillion times per second, if we let our light shine, we can have an enormous affect on all of mankind.

Shining our light brightly explains why prayer can be so effective, especially if there are several people praying for the same thing at the same time.

Just imagine for a moment 570 trillion times per second times a group of 50 people or 100 people. The power behind that prayer is mind blowing. Talk about connection to Source!

For your prayer to be answered, you need to pray the right way. Yes, there is a right way to pray. As Jesus said in Matthew 21:22, "*If you believe you will receive whatever you ask for in prayer.*"

If you want to receive what you are praying for, then you need to pray as if you have already received it. To me, this is true faith. I taught my children to pray as if they have already received what they are praying for, from a place of gratitude.

For example, we pray for their Dad when he is out of town. Our prayer goes like this: *"Thanks for Dad traveling safely and returning home safely."*

According to Guy Finley, author of <u>*The Lost Secrets of Prayer*</u>, every feeling that you are feeling, in every moment, is a request, and every request is a prayer. *Like attracts like.*

You might be saying silently "I'm scared, (i.e. please don't let Dad get hurt traveling), I'm angry, or I'm anxious." The film, *The Secret* shows us, *"Your wish is my command."*

In other words, God/Source is listening. Your request will be fulfilled. Also, according to Guy Finley *"All good things come to those for whom the good is all things."* ***How you perceive is what you'll receive.*** When connected to Source, all is well and good.

Sometimes, I think we get confused about how we are supposed to feel when we are connected to our God/Source. We have often been taught that to be closer to Source, we need to agonize over things, worry or be concerned. Some type of strain, even if only in the expression on your face (veins popping out, lots of intensity), needs to occur. After all, this is serious business.

Let me offer another example from my personal life. My relatives have questioned me about my not demonstrating concern about daily news. In their opinion, my lack of concern means that I don't care about what is happening in the world.

The truth is that I focus on the good that is going on in our world (there really is a lot) because my *request* is for more good. *Focusing upon and requesting good things feels good.*

We have already established: when you feel good, you are connected to Source. Some people think I am just ignorant. The truth is simply that I know the secret to how true connection and prayer for all things to be better really works. Now you have the secret too.

Just smile and be polite when others try to redirect your poor ignorant self to their way of thinking -- concern, worry and agony over things over which none of us has any control. Their intent is good, but misguided.

If you join someone in serious concern for the world, and all that is going wrong in it, then just think what the two of you at 570 trillion times per second can request, *or not request.*

You now know the secret. We definitely have control over where and what we choose to focus our attention upon. In turn, we receive more of that upon which we are focusing.

Mother Teresa was once asked to attend a march against war. She responded, "No, but if you have a march for peace I'll be there." Mother Teresa is definitely someone whose example I follow. I believe she was an authority on the subject of connection to God/Source.

All the greats, such as Jesus, Buddha and Gandhi are examples of connection to Source. They understood the *Law of Attraction* and focused on the good, attracting more good. Jesus said, "Do to others as you would have them do to you." Buddha said, "Consider others as yourself", and Mahatma Gandhi said, "Be the change you want to see in the world."

Follow their lead, and you will soon be an example for others. Jesus said, "And this too you will do, and far more."

The *Law of Attraction* works with prayer, as well as with focus and attention. *A prayer is a response, which is a request. Every feeling or thought is therefore a silent prayer.*

Because every thought or feeling is a silent prayer, becoming conscious of what you are feeling in order to change any negative thoughts *is imperative.* You'll be amazed as you start to receive what you are praying for and ecstatic when what you get is really what you want.

Forgiveness is another very important avenue to becoming connected to your Source. We have touched on forgiveness when we consider that hanging on to anger will literally make you sick.

I have learned, over the years, that there is much more to forgiveness than one would think. Done correctly, forgiveness has a lasting effect, and you will gain a lot for yourself. Not forgiving is one of the biggest and certainly most significant ways to assure your disconnection from God/Source.

You could be doing everything else right, but if you don't forgive then you *alone* will suffer from the lack of forgiveness. The one who you are not forgiving isn't taking the poison, you are. The poison is toxic.

Non-forgiveness stays with all of us 24/7, just like a negative thought. The greasy burger is in and out in a matter of a few hours.

Dr. M. Ted Morter, Jr. writes (page 108) in his book, *The Soul Purpose*: The three steps to forgiveness are:

1. *Self forgiveness.* You must first forgive yourself for allowing the event to affect your health (emotional and/or physical). Forgive yourself for any harm you may have caused yourself because of this situation, action, or person. Literally say, *"I forgive myself for any harm I may have caused myself because of (whomever)."*
2. *Forgive the other person.* Next, you must forgive the other person for any harm he or she may have caused you. Again, literally say these words, *"I forgive (whomever) for any harm he she may have caused me."*
3. *Give the other person permission to forgive you.* It is not necessary or even recommended, that the other person knows that you are taking this step. It is in fact, immaterial. It doesn't

matter whether they know or not, because you are doing this for *you,* not for him or her. The other person may even be deceased and that's okay, too. The forgiveness takes place within *you.* You now say, *"I give (whomever) absolute permission to forgive me for any harm I may have caused him or her."*

I frequently use the following example for my clients, because we can all relate. Have you ever been driving in traffic, and have some cut you off?

1. Forgive yourself for getting upset or angry because another driver cut you off.
2. Forgive the other driver for cutting you off.
3. Give the other driver permission to forgive you for getting angry (perhaps even using a few choice words) at him or her for their rude driving behavior.

Dr. Morter's suggestion for your next step is to *see the good.* Perhaps good in our example might be that you will pay more attention while you are driving, and therefore you will be safer.

The next and very important step in forgiveness: le*arn a lesson from the situation.* The lesson in our on-the-road example may simply be "don't drive like the other driver who cut you off".

Often times the lesson may be that we have no control over how others react, respond, or behave. You might feel great relief with the lesson that we have no control over others—because we are allowing others to own their own stuff. Whew! It's nice to not take on others' stuff as your own, don't you think?

Learning the lesson, in my opinion, is the most important part of forgiveness. When you get something out of a situation, be reminded -- *nothing ever happens to you, it only happens for you.*

When you can see what the *for,* the next step, *be grateful and thankful for the lesson,* is easier.

The last step is let *it go and wish the other person well.* There are a couple of ways that you can check to see if you have successfully completed the forgiveness.

1. Close your eyes and think about the situation. If your face is relaxed and not twitching, and your eyeballs feel still, you have most likely completed the forgiveness successfully.
2. The subject doesn't come up anymore. If the experience continues to come up, perhaps there may be another aspect needing forgiveness. You might need to repeat and continue the forgiveness steps, until you feel the forgiveness is complete.

Forgiving from the heart is most important. Forgiving from the heart will ensure that forgiveness is complete, and forgiveness will not have to be done again.

As you now understand, connecting to your Source/God is one of the most important actions you can take in order to live in a state of love. Connection will move you into love in an instant because God/Source is love.

There are a variety of ways in which to connect. You may already be attempting to connect to Source, but not feeling successful.

Hopefully, the information in this chapter offers you some insight into why connection to Source may not have been made as often or as strongly as desired.

Consciously practice connection. I guarantee that you will feel uplifted and enlightened, and life will become joyful and even fun, when you start to live your life from a place of connection. If you are already living your life with conscious connection to Source, I hope you enjoyed this review, perhaps gaining more insight.

Chapter 4
Who Is the Director of the Movie Titled Your Life?

Slow down you're going too fast. You be the director of this movie called *Your Life*. Let's enjoy *I'm In A Hurry* by Alabama, a song about going too fast.

I'm in a hurry to get things done
(Oh) I rush and rush until life's no fun
All I really gotta do is live and die
But, I'm in a hurry and don't know why

Don't know why
I have to drive so fast
My car has nothing to prove
It's not new, but it'll go 0-60 in 5.2 oh

Can't be late
I leave in plenty of time
Shakin' hands with the clock
I can't stop
I'm on a roll and I'm ready to rock oh,

I hear a voice
It says I'm running behind
I better pick up my pace
It's a race and there ain't no room for someone in 2nd place

I'm In A Hurry describes most of our lives in this society. We have become very fast paced.

Our problem with going so fast all the time is that we miss out on actually enjoying life. We become so exhausted; we can't even tell anyone what we've done in a day.

If you can't slow down, you can't figure out what you want in your life. Before you know it, you're dead.

Both male and female heart attacks are on the rise. I always thought females are the smarter sex. I guess we have all decided that we can't get left behind in this game of life. I think both men and women alike feel the pressure to compete.

Society dictates the criteria by which a person is judged worthy and valued. We are rewarded for working our butts off, and called lazy if we don't.

If your family leaves or gives you money, you are perceived to be less worthy than someone who has "earned" their money. Is the better person the one who struggles? If the comparison between those who earn and those who are *gifted* with money isn't a judgment, I don't know what is.

We spend so much time comparing and competing with each other, we lose our perspective. We don't really know what we want for ourselves anymore.

Our lives are about competition, or meeting certain standards set by society. Ask yourself: "Am I doing what makes me happy, what I am passionate about, or am I just playing *the game*?"

For example, if you think the major corporation for which you are working really values you, you might want to think again.

Following his retirement from a large company, my father-in-law offered some thoughts to my husband. "You are just another number in the company, and if you die tomorrow, they will replace you. It is that simple."

I know how cynical I sound. Unfortunately, I think I have found there is little value placed on employees. Corporations or businesses see their employees simply as resources. The focus is on what you, the employee, can do for the company and not on what the company can do for *you* (the employee).

Wouldn't you rather ask what *you can do for you*? I saw a poster once that said " **RETIREMENT:** *Because You've Given So Much Of Yourself To The Company That You Don't Have Anything Left We Can Use."*

Employees are often let go before they are ready to retire. We read about lay offs all the time. In general it seems corporate America no longer values their employees.

If the employee doesn't feel valued, he or she doesn't have anything to give to the corporation. People who feel valued have a lot to offer the corporation.

For example, let's say I work for a corporation. If I am not valued, I might as well be fired. Were I to stay, I would not benefit from being there, and neither would the company.

Employees get moved around like game pieces, and are let go with no consideration for the value and benefit the worker brings to their position. In my view, this lack of value and consideration are the beginnings of the fall of corporate America.

I personally know a lot of people who have chosen to work for themselves. I say good for those self-employed people -- they value themselves.

A few years ago, I was strictly a "stay at home" Mom. I remember competition between the Moms who stayed home. The conversations went something like this: "Who has it the hardest?" "I have four children and they are two sets of twins." "All of my children are in sports, music, scouting and church programs." "My husband is a pilot and never home." "I have to do it all."

Whenever I mentioned that I (the mother of four) found time for myself and worked out everyday, necks snapped, heads turned fast, jaws dropped, and eyes rolled. I was consistently treated to a chorus of "I'm just too busy to work out."

The looks from the other moms reflected disgust and disappointment. It seemed that I had broken a silent code.

The message, loud and clear: I wasn't a very good mother, because I actually made myself a priority. I wasn't complaining. Instead, I talked about what I did for myself.

To these other Mothers, I wasn't suffering enough to justify myself as a good mother. I thought I was being smart because I took care of myself, and I felt I was a better Mother. I certainly didn't feel as miserable as they sounded.

I never have learned how to compete with other Mothers. My goal is to enjoy being a Mom as much as possible and I look for ways to make parenthood easier.

Oh! Did I say that out loud? Sure hope no one heard me. Actually, I hope you all heard me. *Just because you look for ways to make things easier and enjoy life more doesn't mean that you aren't good at what you do.*

Your approach shows your priorities are straight, and you are probably very good at whatever you do because you are happy while you are doing it.

Doesn't it make sense? If you are happy doing something, then you will naturally do a better job. Having passion for what you're doing guarantees success. If you don't make yourself a priority, nobody else will.

By not making yourself a priority, you will become exhausted, and you won't have the desire or the energy to do anything for anyone else.

Your emotions alone will wipe you out if you don't take care of *you first.* Resentment and bitterness, to name a couple of emotions, will sneak up on you while you're being super Mom or super employee.

Remember, you teach others how to treat you by how you treat yourself. Others follow your lead. If you're a stay at home Mom, for example, and you never take time for yourself, guess what? You're right! You just set yourself up.

You are one against the rest of your family. The family, in turn, very quickly learns that you don't rest, re-energize, or take any vacations. You are on the clock 24/7 and it's okay with you. At the next "Mom competition", you'll win, but so what? I am happy to lose such a competition.

Being the director of your own life means that you do what feels right to you, regardless of what others are doing. Allow others to be the directors of their own movie.

After all, you don't have control over anyone or anything outside of yourself, which should bring you some relief. You can focus on you, and let everyone else do whatever they want to do.

If I had allowed the competitive Moms to influence me, I would surely have joined them in their misery. I could have tried to influence them into my way of thinking, but I knew their choices were none of my business.

I let other moms off the hook by allowing them to live their lives their way. I let myself off the hook by living my life my way. No one *owes* you anything and you don't *owe* anyone else anything. This is true freedom.

We often feel obligated to do for others, or we may *want* to do for others. The truth is *we owe no one*. There is no need to explain and/or justify yourself. The same is true for everyone else as well.

We have been taught that looking out for number one (you) is inconsiderate and selfish. If you do what doesn't feel right to you, then you are living a lie. Doing for others because you feel *obligated* can't feel right or good. *It is important that you live your truth.*

When you make yourself number one, you are able to effortlessly do for others. By allowing your light to shine, you offer an example to encourage others to do the same.

Don't compromise yourself for anyone else. If you do, the compromising will only lead you back into the direction of fear. It is important that you do what you feel is right for you and pursue your dreams.

When you get in your own way, and keep yourself from your true desires, the negative emotions will bombard you and you will be in a total state of fear. Not only will you suffer, but so will everyone else around you.

Relationships quite often make it harder to figure out how to stay true to yourself and your passions, desires and dreams. I don't want to put any pressure on you (okay, yes I do), but ***you are the only one who directs your life!***

You can't blame anyone else. Remember the victim-hood doesn't fit you anymore. **Remember, you are accountable for your own life.** Again, it is vitally important that you don't compromise yourself. I know it's *easier said than done.*

I work on this all the time. With four children and my husband, I have five different relationships in my home. I value each and every one of them.

Since I am a mother, there are certain things that I do for my family. I also make sure I do for myself and my husband and children learn to do for themselves.

I find this approach a win-win situation. I want each of my children to grow up and know they are worthy and can, be, do, and have whatever they want. My children know I care about them, but I do not dictate who they should be, or what they should do or have.

The most important thing to me: my children are happy. By being happy, they will do what they want with passion, and have all that they want, and probably more, in their lives.

Happiness lives towards the end of the maze where love is found. When you are in a place of happiness/love, you are also grateful. Through this state of gratitude, your heart's desires flow to you effortlessly.

People who are really happy and joyful (from the inside out) usually have all that they want in their lives. People are not happy because they have all that they want. Quite the reverse. People have all they want because they are filled with joy and gratitude.

Everyone's heart's desires are different. Each of our desires and dreams are unique to each of us. Your life is a reflection of your individual wants and desires.

Happiness is relative. As I have expressed, having a connection to God/Source is essential in order to create what you want. Your feelings are your best indicator about whether you are connected to Source. Your feelings are also the best way to know if you are in a place to create what you want or not.

There is no need for struggle! Find what brings you joy. You might be thinking, "But won't my children make poor choices, if they are given the room to make their own choices?" Actually, I have found when given room, my children make good choices.

Children are extremely intuitive, and will learn to use their intuition if encouraged and allowed.

According to Albert Einstein, *"The only real valuable thing is intuition."* Remember the children who stayed safe in situations which could have been dangerous? The same intuition will help children direct their own lives.

All you need to do is teach your children about paying attention to how they feel, and how to connect to their Source.

Watch and learn as your children teach you, because they already have the awareness of their own feelings and Source. As a parent, it is important that you recognize your children's *intuitiveness* and continue to remind your children of their ability to know.

Children may not know how to express their intuitive awareness and may say, "Duh, Ma, I already knew that." Wish your children well, and they will be well.

See the good in your children; notice their brilliance, and they will be absolutely *fantabulous!* My husband and I talk a lot to our children. Our children know we don't have our heads in the sand, so there isn't much for our kids to push against.

When children feel there is something to push against, I think they are more likely to get into trouble. In my own high school experience, the kids I knew, who were really into drugs, felt that their parents were really stupid and didn't have a clue.

My parents on the other hand talked to me and my brothers, and I knew they were aware of what teenagers were doing.

Their knowledge took the fun out of doing much, because my parents were already aware. Where was the challenge? There were no threats in regarding the subject of drugs. My parents just conveyed to us their knowledge of teenagers using drugs. There was nothing there to push against. Instead, a door of communication was opened.

What do you expect? Think about this for a moment. Do you think that your expectations play a part in how you are directing your life, or not?

Looking back, I can remember when my husband and I had our first child, our daughter Samantha. We were living in an apartment. A friend couldn't believe that we would have a child before owning a home.

The expectation of much of society is first you have a home, next a baby, in that order. Not the reverse. To other people, I guess we were living life backwards, especially appalling to our friend.

We just didn't have our life in order. Our child was sure to suffer, even though we lived in a two bedroom, two bath apartment. Samantha had her own room and own bathroom. I was puzzled by my friend's attitude. I couldn't figure out what Samantha was going to be missing.

Expectations can be restricting, and take the joy out of life. If my husband Ben and I had the same expectations as my friend, our beautiful Samantha may never have been born.

All we wanted was to love her. By the time Samantha was seven months old, we rented a home. (This still wasn't good enough for my friend.)

We bought our first home when Samantha was 16 months old. You know what? Samantha has never held that against us. Despite the opinions of others about the correct order of buying a house and then raising a baby, everything worked out perfectly for us. Samantha has grown in to a wonderful young woman. So much for the opinions and controlling comments of others about how you should live your life.

Expectations can also be expansive. Expectations can bring more joy to our lives. Look at the United States compared to many other countries. Do you think we citizens of the USA expect a lot -- and therefore, we have a lot? Let me offer another personal, and recent, example.

My family moved almost two years ago from Arizona. When we put the house up for sale, I said I want to sell my house for $500,000 or more. The realtor and my husband both looked at me like I was crazy.

I said, "I **know** what the house is worth, and I expect to sell it for what it is worth." Both Ben and the realtor tried to convince me to lower the price. I wouldn't go lower than $499,999.

We were short on time. We needed to be moved and settled into our new home no later than late July, because school was scheduled to start in mid-August. We were already moving past June.

We had an unadvertised open house on a Saturday. Fifty different families visited and looked through our home. The house sold within one week-end of being placed on the market. You guessed it. We received over $500,000 for our home -- $512,500, to be exact.

Our home sold for $90,000 more then the most recently sold home in the neighborhood. I think that our realtor was in disbelief. He just kind of shook his head at me and said, "Well I guess you got what you wanted!" Yes I did! I never had any doubt, and I expected an excellent outcome.

The story doesn't stop here though. While we were on the road, moving to Colorado, our Colorado realtor called with news.

"There is a problem with the appraisal." We agreed to pay one price for our new home, and two appraisals came back $10,000 too low. Because of the low appraisals, the bank was likely to reject our loan application, making us unable to purchase the Colorado home.

Our Colorado realtor was able to get another appraisal, which miraculously came back at exactly our offer, creating a red flag for us. Something was terribly wrong with the appraisals.

Our mortgage loan officer strongly encouraged us to get an additional "unbiased" appraisal separate from both realtors. We did. This fourth appraisal came back low also.

In the mean time, we were on the road and our furniture and belongings were too, heading to Colorado without a home to call our own.

My husband's back went out because of the stress, and I was deciding how things were going to turn out. I told my husband very excitedly about what was going to happen.

"We're going to get the house for less than the original price, a lot less, and everyone is going to walk away happy." I was sure that the sellers would meet us somewhere in the middle because they wanted to sell as badly as we wanted to buy.

Sure enough, the next day a phone call resounded with the good news: we bought our house for $6,000 less than the asking price. My husband just looked at me and said, "How do you do that?"

I just decide what I want. I imagine it, see it and feel it. Next, **I expect it**. Because the experience feels so real, what I expect must also be real. Then, I *allow* it to happen (this is where most people get stuck). I never look for reasons for why my expectations can't happen.

I know it sounds juvenile and naïve, but recall my observations about children and their connection to Source. What appears to be juvenile and naïve may also mean I am functioning at a higher level.

My natural tendency is to go upward, when someone else might take a nose dive, crash and burn. I am human. As a human, I sometimes get off track for a short time. I get back on track fairly quickly when I remember what it is I want.

Notice experiences, desires and results of wants and desires in your life. Notice how results seem to be equal to your personal passion about your wants and desires.

If you are perhaps feeling lukewarm, and not terribly invested, meaning you don't *feel* very strongly about what it is you say you want, the occurrence or results are pretty much equal to your lukewarm attitude and emotions. Likely, no dramatic results will occur because no passion was invested in the desire. Consider your clarity about what you want and desire.

With change comes opportunity. Life is movement and change. Thus, life is opportunity. I can always see the upside of a situation, and the upside is where my attention goes.

My attention is focused on where I'm going. Perhaps I might be incredibly abnormal by most people's standards, but my reality is a happy one.

Let's get back to our home purchase. The loan officer, who encouraged us to get another appraisal separate from the two realtors, shared some interesting news after all the paper work was signed.

She said the appraiser whose appraisal came back at exactly the asking price had come into her office and said he owed our realtor a favor. Our loan officer was appalled at this statement.

My assumption is the appraiser set the value of the house at exactly the asking price in order to help close the deal for our realtor. Grounds for dismissal, I am sure!

Our loan officer wanted to give us a heads up, but the best she could do was to encourage us to get another appraisal. I believe that her phone call urging us to get another appraisal would not have occurred if I hadn't been focused on such a great outcome. The phone call wouldn't fit with a negative outcome. I am the director of the movie called ***My Life.***

Are you starting to get this director stuff now? I know Hollywood makes it look difficult, but this is **your life.** If you allow yourself to follow your passions, desires and dreams, your life will be fun and easy.

Shake off your negative thoughts and energies. Get yourself present and focused in the moment. Create a picture of what you want your life to look like.

If you're happy with the way your life is going, what else do you want, or want to do with your life? Life keeps moving, even if you're happy.

Chop, chop! Let's get with it. The journey isn't over just because you think that you have everything you want, and you are where you want to be.

Life is not about getting finished. Life is about *the journey.* You never get finished anyway. Who wants to do nothing when there is always something to do?

If you want to do nothing, then you might as well just lie down and die. I'd rather see you *do something.* (Just a reminder: in my opinion, when you do die, you probably won't be "doing nothing" then, either. You'll just be experiencing existence differently and it will be wonderful.)

The following dream regarding my father gives an example of what *I* mean by "existing differently" after death, or more commonly referred to as "life after death".

After my Dad died (just over a year ago) I had a dream. In my dream, my Dad took me to a place where he was painting a purple wall. While on this planet, my Dad never did anything even close to painting. It just wasn't his thing.

I asked Dad, "What are you doing?" He said, "I'm painting." "I see, but why?" I responded. Seeing him paint was so strange to me.

"Because I can, and I like it." He answered with a smile and a tone of entitlement and worthiness.

Spiritually, I believe that we go on forever. Once we leave our physical bodies, we continue on and on, and so does the fun. We have even more fun, in most cases, because we are no longer in our own way.

What's next? If you are feeling pretty good about where you are, then you are in a great position to direct your life further. Look at what you have already accomplished! You can see how good you are at direction. Maybe all you want to do now is to learn something new. Whatever you choose, have fun.

Chapter 5
The Force Is with You

In the words of the Jedi, "The force is with you." George Lucas, in an interview with Bill Moyers, expressed his views: *"Ultimately the force is the larger mystery of the universe. And to trust your feelings is your way into that.* ***Using the Force*** *is a leap of faith. There are mysteries and powers larger than we are, and you have to* ***trust your feelings*** *in order to access them."*

The power is within you to be the director of your life. You need your thoughts and emotions to match your heart's desire. Only in matching your desires, thoughts and feelings, can you manifest what you truly want in your life.

If you are angry, for example, you won't be able to move in the direction towards love. Anger, as we've already seen, is one of our most debilitating emotions. Rage will bounce you around like a loose ping pong ball and set you off into an uncontrolled spin.

It is okay to be angry. You need to *move out* of anger and up to something else that feels better, as soon as possible! *Anger can be very debilitating if you stay there too long, but at the same time, anger can be a very powerful kick in the butt into action.*

When you fight against a feeling, you just generate more of the feeling you are fighting against.

Allow your anger. Work through the anger (i.e., experience forgiveness). You will likely gain incredible insight and move faster towards where you would rather be.

Guilt is another emotion stopping you very quickly from moving forward in the movie script of your life. You could have the whole script written and published. Yet guilt can blow the whole deal for you in an instant.

What a waste! Guilt, in my opinion, is the same as self-pity. Think about how people express guilt. Someone may say things like "I guess if I hadn't taken time to go for a walk today, the laundry would have been done." Or, "It's because I said, or did what I did, that my children (or spouse) haven't ever accomplished what they wanted to." "If I were just a better mother (or wife) my children (or spouse) would have done better in life."

Wow, guilt gives you a lot of power. *Or not.* You do not have the power to make anyone feel any particular way. If someone feels bad because of something you say or do, he or she is responsible for giving their power away.

My husband Ben used to think that he was responsible for my happiness. I finally told him to get over himself. Ben is not in control of my happiness. I am in control of my happiness. What an ego. He got over his ego and feelings of guilt and responsibility regarding *my* happiness a long time ago. Ben now pays attention to his own happiness, and does so quite well, I might add. It took a little getting used to, but we are both empowered and free to be responsible for our *own* happiness. We feel happy when we are together. I believe this is a good thing!

Guilt will keep us from joy, because we often feel there are more important things we should be doing. Perhaps, for example, we should be cleaning our homes or fixing our fences.

Don't sabotage your right to a joyful life. Give up the guilt! Enjoying yourself is more important than house cleaning any day. You'll know when it is time to take care of the little details of life. In the meantime, focus on joy!

Here I go again, encouraging you to be selfish. If you aren't selfish enough to be in joy as much as possible, then you will stay stuck in the muck and be asking yourself, "What the f---?, is this all there is to life?"

You should be able to celebrate every waking moment. Remember the lesson from the dog or a child? Taking care of yourself doesn't mean that you are irresponsible.

Find a way to enjoy life as much as possible. Once and for all, ***let go of any guilt*** due to the fact that you have found a way to be happy and content without struggle.

Often it seems that guilt is related to things going well without a struggle. *It is okay* to have things go well without a struggle. Really it is. I am not aware of any rule stating the only way you can get to joy is through struggle.

Take the easy way out. Have fun just because you can. Paint just because you can, and because you like it. Don't wait until you're dead.

Experience heaven right here on earth. Remember, you have a safety net waiting to let you know if you are out of line. You will feel bad if you need to abstain from your current behavior. Stay tuned in to your joy. Have a great time without any guilt.

Depression is an emotion very close to the end of the maze where fear lives. Depression is even closer to fear than anger and guilt. When you are in a depression, you may feel paralyzed. You don't move.

With anger and guilt, you are still active. When you are depressed you just do nothing, which is pretty close to dead. Other people may often be okay with your being depressed, at least for a while. Depressed people are quiet, do not complain, and are not in the way.

My own experience with depression might be a good example. I know that my husband felt more at peace when I was depressed regarding our finances, than he did when I got angry. It was easier for him when I wasn't in his face. Imagine having a pet turtle verses a pet dog. A depressed person needs to be watered and fed, but does not want to be played with, and certainly does not want to be entertained. The problem: nothing happens until the depressed person decides to get mad and then he or she moves. This is what happened to me when we had financial problems.

I stayed in bed for a while. Then I got pissed, and soon after, I found the answer I was looking for.

Another problem with depression; a depressed person often bounces back and forth between anger and depression. Depressed people simply do not know where else to go. Either we have not been taught to move above anger, or we don't know how. Some of us may never have ventured from anger toward love before.

Moving out of anger is unfamiliar territory. If you can get yourself *pissed off and blame* someone else, at least you are moving.

Next, get yourself to where you just feel *frustrated*. Keep moving on up, and eventually you'll move forward to *hopefulness*. If you can move forward to hopefulness, you can likely get to *joy* and fall right into *love*.

Once you experience feelings, such as anger, frustration and hopefulness, in this progressive order, you are likely to remember your progress the next time you need to move out of depression. As you go through this process of moving up from depression to love, remember that **you are worthy!!! Say it our loud. I AM WORTHY! I AM WORTHY! I AM WORTHY!**

As you remember your worthiness, you will spend less and less time being depressed. Self-education is often the key. Seek out some good information.

Research suggested readings, movies, informative web sites and healing techniques. You will thrive and your life will expand.

What a beautiful thing. Watch closely. Before long, you won't recognize yourself. Can I get a Halleluiah? I'm sure that's what you'll be saying, because your relief will be great.

Envy and jealousy are two more emotions directing you into fear. Envy is all about wanting what you don't have, and experiencing negative feelings and negative thoughts towards the person who does have what you want. Jealousy is all about fear of losing something or someone, and experiencing negative feelings and negative thoughts over the anticipated loss. More often than not it has to do with relationships. For example, the fear is of losing a girlfriend or boyfriend to another person.

Truly monstrous, envy and jealousy are *so* ugly. Both emotions are similar to anger, because anger and resentment are neatly wrapped up within the emotional envy/jealousy package.

If you are envious or jealous of someone, I highly doubt that you are having warm thoughts toward them. More than likely, you are feeling resentment because you perceive the other person possesses what you want or view them as a threat to you.

I think the emotions of envy, jealousy, anger and resentment are the reasons why people who don't have money often decide that people who do have money aren't good people.

Here are some judgments envious people make against the people of whom they are envious. 1) The good people are the ones who are working hard and don't have money. (I guess having less makes you somehow morally better and you earn the *virtuous award* because you have more insight, or some crapola like that.) 2) You've been through stuff that those "rich" people could never relate to. 3) You can understand the down and out where they can't. (Rich people cannot relate to down and out even if they wanted to, and they do not want to because they are cold hearted.) 4) Rich people only care about themselves.

Wow! Notice the judgments being passed out by the "better person". Do you hear it? Think about what envy sounds and looks like. Poison arrows are flying all over the place. Envy, one of the ugliest emotions, is not justified.

The one who has what you want usually isn't even aware of the ugliness you are sending their way. People who are objects of another's envious and negative thoughts are often functioning at a high level, and do not feel the negativity sent their way.

Have I burst the envious person's balloon? Sorry for screwing up pity parties. The truth: envious people are wasting valuable energy that should be directed toward improving their own lives.

If you are envious of someone else, study their approach to see how that person has achieved what you want. Learn, and be grateful he or she is in your life.

I am not suggesting you do everything that they do. Learn from their actions, and apply what you like to your own life. No one else needs to know what you are doing.

Albert Einstein said *"The secret to creativity* is *knowing how to hide your sources."* You can take all the credit for your success. When you realize what a gift the other person is to you, the envy should subside. Perhaps you may even feel some gratitude and even happiness for the other person's participation in your life.

Even when you start out feeling a negative emotion like depression, you can be guided by someone else, or you guide yourself (through self talk) into feeling better about your situation. Eventually, you move forward, and end up closer to the side of the maze where love thrives.

How fast you move from depression to love is a very individual process. A lot of details come into play as you travel on your path from depression to love or joy.

For example, how long have you been depressed? Can you remember a time when you felt joyful?

If you have been stuck in the muck of depression for a long time, depression has become familiar. Because depression is familiar, it becomes your comfort zone, in the sense that depression is all you know.

I wouldn't necessarily expect a depressed person to go right into feeling hopeful. Let's revisit my own depression. When I was depressed (not the norm for me) about my finances years ago, I got angry, and then vengeful, before I was able to move anywhere else.

I went through several different emotions before I got to gratitude and thankfulness. I bounced around between a lot of emotions while I tried to practice gratitude, as a way to get back to love and joy.

I went from depression to anger, to guilt, to doubt, to feeling overwhelmed, to hopeful, and back to overwhelmed. This wild ride was only for starters! I also experienced frustration, back to anger, up to contentment, to boredom, and up to optimism.

When I finally received an answer about how to get out of the trouble we were in, I felt hopeful and even happy. What a huge relief!

I was able to start moving up towards better feelings. When I felt empowered, I felt freedom. Freedom brought me into joy and love again. Empowerment equals freedom. What a journey.

If you are doing something because you are threatened, and you *feel* something bad will happen if you don't take action, then you are living in fear. You are trying to *prevent* something from happening.

When you are trying to *prevent something from happening*, you are focused on it. You attract what you are focused on like a magnet (law of attraction). You bring what you are focused on right to you. What you focus on expands, and becomes more.

Perhaps you are focusing on something good, or on something bad. Your focus will cause whatever you are focusing on to show up more in your life.

For example, let's say you are exercising to prevent a heart attack from occurring (because heart attacks run in your family). You are actually in fear of having a heart attack. Your focus is on having a heart attack.

Exercise because exercising *feels* good. You will feel good if you exercise. *Feeling good feels good.*

If you are eating healthy foods because you don't want to get fat or sick, you are in fear of getting fat or sick. Your focus is on getting fat or sick. Instead, eat healthy foods because you *feel* more energetic when you eat healthier. Feeling more energetic feels good.

Life's journey is all about feeling better in order to connect to your Source/God, which is love. You will enjoy this life journey of yours so much more when you achieve your personal connection to Source/God.

From my perspective, the journey is the most important part of the ride, because the destination is death. I think the experience or state of being which we call death should be cool, too, but while I have this body to run around in, my intent is to enjoy the ride.

Personally, I don't think this is the last ride I'll be taking. I don't know if I will have memories of this journey, so while I am here, I am sure of one thing. I want to experience this life from a place of love and joy as much as humanly possible.

As George Lucas says, "*You've got to trust your feelings,*" in order to access "*The Force*" within each and all of us. As you go through different feelings and emotions, allow the internal, intuitive part of you to lead you naturally up and out of fear, towards love and joy.

Remember: begin with the attitude of gratitude. Thinking about and feeling what you are grateful and thankful for is a fantastic way to start in the right direction.

Consider the example of envy. See that you can be grateful when the person who has what you want shows up in your life. Instead of being envious, you can perhaps feel *optimistic.*

Sound like a leap? If you see someone who has obtained what you want, you can notice methods by which you can accomplish the same goals as well. Take my recent experience as an example.

I know someone currently applying for a position within her company. I'll call her Linda (not her real name). Linda's heart's desire is to work remotely, so she can live where she wants.

Linda is aware of employees in other companies who work remotely. She feels some envy. Just recently, Linda discovered a fellow employee, we'll call him John, who applied for and received a position in which he can work remotely. He is living wherever he desires.

Linda's initial envy eventually subsided, replaced with an optimistic attitude. Linda can see that she too can make this happen for herself.

Really, this process is all a matter of staying tuned in, present and focused in the moment. If you can stay tuned in, be present and focused, you won't miss the things helping you to head toward love and joy, instead of being stuck in fear feelings.

For example, if Linda wasn't looking for ways to feel more optimistic or hopeful, she probably would have missed the information about her fellow employee who achieved what he wanted—a job allowing him to work remotely.

The information about John helped Linda on the path towards feeling better. At the same time, she could have just gone into more envy over the fact that John had exactly what he desired. Wallowing in her envy could have caused Linda to miss what was actually good news for her.

The fact of the matter: there is plenty of good stuff to go around. No shortage on the good stuff! Wake up and smell the roses.

You have to feel to heal, and if you resist it will persist. I have this written on my business cards. You definitely do have to feel and not resist in order to heal.

I don't think there is any way around it—feeling is connected to healing. What if you are on medication and you don't feel the medication will help you?

For example, if you don't *feel* that the medication can work, then guess what -- it won't. You have to *believe* and *feel* what you are doing works in order for healing to take place.

Your feelings are your way to *"The Force"* or your Source/God. Your feelings give you your road map through the maze to love.

Learning how to direct your thoughts, by paying attention to how you are feeling, is essential to obtaining personal freedom and power. I think the only goal any of us should really have in life is to live in joy and love.

If living in joy and love is our goal, we need to vigilantly be looking at whether or not our feelings are working toward this goal. Let each of us make this attention to our thoughts and feelings a habit.

Mahatma Gandhi said, "*Your beliefs become your thoughts, your thoughts become your words, your words become your actions, your actions become your* ***habits,*** *your* ***habits*** *become your values, your values become your destiny.*"

It is very difficult to monitor every waking thought. It's not difficult to pay attention to how you feel. Make it simple and check: good feelings or bad feelings.

In *Journey from Fear to Love,* I have given you several strategies to start on the path and move towards feeling better. Apply whatever works for you.

Eckhart Tolle, author of The Power of Now, wrote "*When you live in complete acceptance of what is, that is the end of all drama in your life.*"

I think his view applies here about feelings. Tolle's view relates to first acknowledging your feelings and being okay with having these feelings.

We must first acknowledge our feelings in order to be able to move on and up towards something better. Acceptance of your feelings is the first step to healing.

When you accept your feelings, drama diminishes. Your goal is not to drag around these negative emotions. Previously, dragging around the negative emotions may have been your goal. You may have been using these emotions for some pay off such as attention or as an excuse.

Instead, you have now arrived at an understanding about why these emotions have shown up. You can now move closer to love, as soon as possible.

Start by always having your goal of living in joy and love in the forefront of your mind. Become like the six million dollar man. Be built better, faster, stronger than ever before as you greatly increase your ability to move from negative emotions, right back into joy and love.

You won't be faking it! You will be using the tools you have to help you remember that love and joy are really what life is all about. Not only is it okay to feel loving, joyful and happy, it is beyond okay! Living in love and joy is the only thing that makes perfect sense.

Chapter 6
Believing Is Seeing

Young children understand the idea that believing is seeing. Their eyes light up on Christmas morning, or when they discover the treasure the tooth fairy left under their pillow.

Children don't question whether or not Santa exists, or if the tooth fairy is real. They believe, and therefore they see. Adults can learn so much from children! We think, however, children need to learn so much from us.

If we (adults) could just be still for a while, and really pay attention to how children live their lives, we could receive a true and new education. This education would be very valuable and empowering.

The diploma earned: *freedom*. Freedom definitely lives on the end of the maze where love thrives.

By now, you may be wondering, "How can you compare a child's life to an adult's life? Making believe about Santa or the tooth fairy just doesn't compare to the reality of an adult's life."

My point precisely! Lighten up. Maybe you don't believe in Santa or the tooth fairy anymore, but what do they really represent? Santa and the tooth fairy represent *love, fun and joy.*

The reason parents go out of their way to share Santa and the tooth fairy with their children is *precisely because* these delightful characters represent love, fun and joy.

Maybe you can't see love, fun and joy in your life right now, but if you believe love, fun and joy exist, you will soon enjoy this amazing trio of experiences and feelings.

You must also believe that you are *worthy* of love, fun and joy. Generally, children do feel worthy. Of course they deserve to have Santa and the tooth fairy visit their homes!

Even if Santa and the tooth fairy are "just pretend", can you see and remember how real they are to a child? Believing is seeing. Believing is creating and attracting.

The belief in a child's heart, in this case Santa's visit, can be so powerful that sometimes a child can attract a good hearted a stranger to make Santa's gifts a reality, even if the child's parents are unable to afford gifts. We often hear stories about a Good Samaritan who gave a family or a child Christmas presents from Santa. I wonder what the children who received such gifts might have said if I had been able to interview them. I suspect I would have discovered what the children knew in their hearts and truly believed -- that *Santa would indeed come.*

Do you think the children's pure, untainted *belief* in Santa's arrival had anything to do with the fact of his *actual* arrival? I do. The law of attraction is always working.

Can you see how you could apply the law of attraction to your grown up life?

Children believe. Children have no doubt, and they get what they want. I can remember as a child really wanting a certain pair of shoes. I looked at the pictures of those shoes, and thought about them.

I never said anything to my parents. We didn't ask for much, because as children, we didn't receive a lot of extra things.

Even though I never asked for or even mentioned the shoes, the next time my Mom and I went shopping, I miraculously got the very shoes I wanted.

I was always very grateful, but I never told Mom how much I really wanted those shoes. You can do the same thing with adult stuff, too. Recall my real estate experience.

Remember how we sold our home in Arizona? I believed with all of my heart that I would sell my house for over $500,000, even when everyone around me basically said that I was nuts.

I remember intensely believing and feeling the sale for over that amount. I saw it happen in my mind, and the sale became a reality (to the dismay of everyone else involved).

Their vision of what could happen was based on the fact that the last house sold in the neighborhood closed at $90,000 less. If you are waiting to 1) see *first;* and 2) *believe after* you see, you are holding yourself up.

Don't base your believing on someone else showing you *first,* in order for you to first see, and then believe. Instead, *you be the example* for someone else. Believe first, and enjoy what you see become your reality.

The beauty of believing and seeing: as long as *you are believing and seeing with feeling,* it doesn't matter what anyone else is doing.

In other words, your believing and seeing is a very personal thing. No one else can mess it up for you. The reverse is also true. You can't mess up believing and seeing for anyone else.

Believing and seeing is truly wonderful, empowering and freeing. If you believe it and see it with feeling, you can literally make it happen. Like the Nike commercial, *"Just do it."*

Perhaps you are wondering if you can *do it wrong*, or if you are breaking any rules. No. You can't make something happen if it doesn't feel good. Therefore, you aren't going to create something bad.

Bad things might still happen, but not because of something that *you are doing.* On the contrary, you might attract something unwanted because of something that you *are not doing, such* as not *focusing* on what it is that you want to come into your life. You are instead believing and seeing all kinds of things that you don't necessarily want in your life.

For example, perhaps you may watch the news, and believe and see that the bad news is everywhere around you. ("The flu is just waiting to get you next.") Whether or not you are *conscious of your belief* that you will get the flu, you see it happening to you, and you indeed will be the next to get it. I know it seems too simple to be true. You may say, "Life just can't be that simple." Believe me, it is!

People make life much more complicated than it is. We complicate life with all kinds of reasons or *excuses* for why things go the way they do in our lives.

The truth is you get what you get because of your own beliefs. Your results have nothing to do with anyone else. All of what you have in your life has been an *inside job.*

You express what is inside you, and what is inside you is what you see in your life. Like it or not, that is just the way it is. You can't hold anyone or anything else responsible for the results you see and experience.

Isn't that great news? I think so. *Use the same power which you used to create your current experience, in order to change what you have created.*

Wow! You are the artist of your life. If you don't like your life, you can wipe off the canvas and start over. You are your own boss. Creating is similar to building a house. Lay a great foundation: *you are being your worthy self.*

You may discover you don't like the décor, windows, floors or walls. You can decide to live with your creation, and be unhappy, or you can start to remodel.

You don't need to move because the foundation is solid, and the neighborhood (the uniqueness of you) is great. All you need to do is change it up a little. Do some *updating and complimenting by* building upon the solid foundation and the great neighborhood.

If I were you, my next question would be, "Where the heck did these dang beliefs come from anyway?" Beliefs create your thoughts. Thoughts create your feelings. Feelings create your actions or lack of actions.

Your beliefs color how you perceive your life. I remember hearing something as a child. People who are looking at the good in the world and not the bad are looking through rose colored glasses.

I think this view is actually supposed to be an insult. Wouldn't it be nice if life were that easy? If each of us looked at each other through rose colored glasses, the world would look very pretty. I do think if people could all see the good instead of the bad in the world (the effect of rose colored glasses), the problems of the world could be solved.

What would we have to fight over? *It's all good.* Everyone would be okay with where they are in their lives.

The beauty of looking at the world through rose colored glasses is your own positive contribution to your overall health, without drugs and alcohol. This happy experience is better than drugs or alcohol. We would all be naturally high, because our perceptions would be instantly altered. Wow! Perhaps rose colored glasses could solve the major problems of drug and alcohol abuse going on all over the world. Perhaps I should have a career in politics, campaigning for rose colored glasses. Do you think people are ready? Not yet.

According to Dr. Bruce Lipton, in *The Biology of Belief, Unleashing The Power of Consciousness, Matter, and Miracles,* *"In fact, those rose-colored glasses are necessary for your cells to thrive. Positive thoughts are a biological mandate for a happy, healthy life."*

In his book, Dr. Lipton also explains the origin of negative beliefs. According to Dr. Lipton, between birth and two years old, the brain operates mostly at the lowest EEG frequency, 0.5 to 4 cycles per second (Hz), known as Delta waves.

(EEGs stand for electroencephalograms, which are defined as electric head pictures. These head pictures show a graded range of brain activity in human beings.)

A child between two and six years of age spends more time at a higher EEG level which is characterized as Theta (4Hz - 8 Hz).

In order to hypnotize patients, hypnotherapists drop their adult client's brain activity into Delta and Theta. The low frequency brain waves place patients into a more suggestible, programmable state.

"Young children carefully observe their environment and download the worldly wisdom offered by parents directly into their subconscious

memory. As a result, their parents' behavior and beliefs become their [the children's] own."

The behaviors, beliefs and attitudes we observed in our parents were programmed into our subconscious mind. Can we blame everything on our parents?

Blaming your parents will get you no where, except into the "hood" of "victim-hood". It is important for you to you recognize where your beliefs come from. Don't let this awareness stop you from moving forward.

The "hood" is attached to a very long lead lined cape. The lead lined cape feels like a very heavy load. Not a fun place to hang out!

When I get a picture in my head of someone wearing this "victim- hood" and cape I see the grim reaper. The grim reaper is an appropriate picture, because being a victim really does suck the life out of you.

According to Dr. Lipton, *"The subconscious is our "autopilot" and the conscious mind is our "manual control."* Dr. Lipton also notes: the subconscious mind processes 20 million environmental stimuli per second. The conscious mind processes 40 environmental stimuli per second.

The subconscious runs the show. We are basically wired with the beliefs we picked up from our parents when we were young and easily programmed.

Children can be easily brain washed. A child's brain is functioning at a level which can be easily hypnotized. The child's brain is in a more suggestible, programmable state than an adult's brain. Children, therefore, are more easily controlled.

Also according to Dr. Lipton, a child's consciousness has not evolved enough to evaluate and discern that what the child is observing, or being told by parents, may not be the truth about themselves or their environment (or, as he writes, "not necessarily true characterizations of 'self'").

Once programmed into the subconscious mind, the information which the child has received, and what the child has observed becomes their "truth". This "truth" shapes and defines the child's behavior and potential through life.

For example, let's say a child is informed that he or she is worthless or stupid. Sadly, the "worthless or stupid" message is downloaded into the subconscious memory. The current and future life of the child will surely to reflect the cruel message.

Jeff, a friend of mine, was always told as a child he was not as smart, musically inclined or athletic as his older sibling. Jeff struggled with school, gave up music and never attempted any sports.

To this day Jeff judges himself very harshly in everything he does. He is his own worst critic.

His older sibling, Janice, was always told she was too heavy. To this day, she is obsessed with her weight.

Another friend of mine, Amy, was told as a child she was "slow". She ended her education at high school, and has never tried to advance in her place of employment.

Amy compares herself to others all the time, with the explanation: "It's because I don't have an education." The "it" is everything she considers a failure in her life.

You can see how your beliefs may restrict your life dramatically!

Dr. Lipton further explains the power of the subconscious. Let's consider this example. A preprogrammed behavior takes place, controlled by the subconscious mind. The conscious mind is observing, *and can stop* the preprogrammed behavior. A different response can then be created by the conscious mind.

For example, let's say you have a preprogrammed behavior about money. You are preprogrammed to feel you never have enough. You go into a panic when an unexpected expense shows up, such as a car repair.

The conscious mind can take over and help get you settled down for the moment. You might say to yourself, "I have the money in the bank to cover the repairs. By having the repairs taken care of now, maybe I'll avoid any further damage to the car."

The problem we all face is *the subconscious mind takes over the moment the conscious mind isn't paying attention.* The conscious mind has the ability to think forward and backward in time. The subconscious mind functions only in the present moment.

Our conscious mind creates our own thoughts, aspirations, happy thoughts, dreams and desires. Our conscious mind plans for a bright future. Our subconscious mind's behaviors, on the other hand, may not be coming out of our own creations. Most subconscious behaviors were programmed when we were children.

Using our example of money, you might be able to stop the preprogrammed behavior for a moment. Since the subconscious belief about money is a preprogrammed behavior, the underlying beliefs (programmed in the subconscious mind) are still present.

Remember and be aware: our subconscious beliefs can override the conscious mind the moment our conscious mind is not alert and paying attention. Being present and focused as often as possible is very helpful while traveling on this journey from fear to love.

If you are not paying attention to your preprogrammed beliefs when the car breaks down, the subconscious can take over. You could end up in a total panic over the car repair!

You might not even repair the car because your subconscious sends you into fear about spending the money. Not repairing the car could prevent you from going to work. You could lose your job. The domino effect takes over.

I'm exaggerating a little with this example, but not much. People really do have such responses due to subconscious programming. If we are not aware, we can not use our conscious mind to stop the subconscious behavior. Good old will power *can* work. How exhausting to use will power all the time!

If we only had programmed behaviors in the subconscious mind such as abundance, worthiness, well-being and overall health, we could have incredibly "fantabulous" lives without ever having to involve our conscious mind.

Dr. Lipton comments, *"We could be totally successful in our lives without ever having to be conscious."* I'm all for that. How about you?

Let's talk about how we can fill the subconscious mind with all of these wonderful, positive thoughts.

First off, ask yourself: are you ready to open up to the wonderful world already waiting for you? I think you are indeed ready.

First, you likely need to make space. Clean up the extra "stuff" holding you back. The magnificence of who you are needs space to fully show up 100% in the now.

This next step requires you to get yourself out of your own way. *The "hood" (victim-hood) has to go.* You are now fully accountable for your own life.

Do you think you can take the heat? You have to own all of your life. Be accountable for what you like and don't like about where your life is today.

Your life is all about *you, and you alone*. Your accountability can be viewed as really good news. You don't have to give a rip about what anyone else has to say about what you're doing or not doing.

We are taking this to the inside Source, which is **you!** If you're ready (and you are), get in the driver's seat for a great ride. Buckle up! Get ready and enjoy the best ride in the park.

Perhaps a good place to start would be identifying, for yourself, the parts of your life which are upsetting. For example, are you happy or depressed? Do you have pain or illness in your body?

Are you experiencing great abundance in your life, or do you feel lack in all or some aspects of your life? In which areas do you feel lack?

Take some time to quietly reflect and see what *you* can identify as "problem(s)" for you. Perhaps you might seek a counselor to help you confirm your perceptions are on target. Or, you might seek practitioner who will work *with you,* to help you identify your issues for yourself.

I'm not knocking counseling. Counseling is often a good place to start. (My background is in counseling.) However, counseling is sometimes more a *"do to"* therapy then a *"do with"* therapy.

The counselor typically tells the client what *to do*, (similar to techniques such as massage, reiki, or acupuncture). The client experiences something done *to* them.

We have arrived together at a wonderful point in *Fear to Love.* I would truly rather see you go to a practitioner who will work *with you* and make the session a *cooperative effort.*

I know some counselors do use additional techniques (along with counseling), allowing the client to discover their priorities *through their own being.* The counselor works together with the client.

In my opinion, a counselor who works *with you* to help you discover your priorities, *through your own being*, is a good counselor with whom to work.

If you feel you need confirmation from an outside source, simultaneous counseling plus a technique in which *your being* is a tool in the process is a good idea. Let me explain.

I use a couple of techniques for myself, and I supplement with massage. The massage therapist confirms the healing techniques I am using are making positive changes in my physical body.

The massage also helps my body tremendously with the healing process. I know if I weren't doing the inside work first, the massage would not have the same healing effect.

My healing progress simply would not be the same. Though some of my being might heal indefinitely, new problems could still continue to arise.

I believe by doing the inside work and massage simultaneously, I am able to heal at the deepest level of my being. Also, my massage therapist happens to be really knowledgeable and very good, actually beyond good. Diane is exceptional.

She uses energy work while doing massage. Before Diane even starts working with a client she asks the universe to support her as she assists her client in the healing process.

She also sends healing thoughts to each of her clients as she works with them. Diane's intent is always to help facilitate healing for everyone with whom she works. Basically, Diane takes massage up a few levels. Diane teaches her clients how to take care of themselves by teaching specific stretches to be done at home. Actually a "do with" massage therapist, Diane still needs you to do the inside work in order to have her therapy be as beneficial as possible.

I truly believe trying to heal or move forward and expand, without dealing with the *stuff* stored in the subconscious or your emotions, will only give you a temporary fix. The present symptoms may go away, but new symptoms will show up if you skip the vital step of clearing emotions and the subconscious "stuff".

If not dealt with, negative emotions or beliefs will continue to get in your way. Remember: the subconscious runs the show. The root cause of every issue or problem you have has to do with your beliefs, thoughts, feelings and emotions.

What you eat doesn't affect your health as much as your emotions-- what you believe and how you feel. Your beliefs and feelings are with you all the time, 24 hours a day, seven days a week. The food, *well shit,* just isn't with you 24 hours a day. Food, once digested, and negative emotions all result in shit (quite a pile). The *pile* of negative emotions is the most damaging.

Your nutrition is not as important as how you feel. Nutrition doesn't have the same long term affect on you, and therefore it is not as damaging.

Your emotions and feelings are with you *all the time.* People think eating right and exercising is all it takes to be healthy. The real deal is your emotions can override your good eating habits and make you sick anyhow.

Feelings are more powerful than food. One of my many teachers told me a story about a (much older) man, extremely healthy, who lived on beef, and potatoes or French fries. He was also one of the most joyful people that she had ever met. Conversely, you can be the healthiest eater and still become sick because the root cause of everything, as I have said, is feelings.

We are not consciously aware of the root causes of our difficulties, which are stored in our subconscious memories. The reason I am reiterating this point is to make sure you understand my opinion.

Due to my own personal and professional experiences, I believe it is critical for you to make changes. *Use your own being* as the gauge for what changes you need to make.

I wouldn't want to see you making changes based on what *another person tells you* to do. Remember: *this is an inside job.*

If you go outside of yourself to figure out what you need to do, you give your power away. The journey then becomes about what other people think.

Do you see how other people controlling your life doesn't fit in with the themes of this book? We don't give a flying hoot about what other people think.

I'm offering strategies for *you to become empowered.* True, "do to" therapies can point you in the right direction. I hope, by now, you are ready to get in the driver's seat and take control of your own life.

The bottom line is *the only way to you is through you. You* hold all the answers to all of *your* questions and all of your issues or problems. The power really does lie *within you.*

I know I promised a great ride. Here it goes. Although several techniques are out there to help you get to the root causes of your problems, I am going to talk to you about my top two choices.

My top two choices will enlighten you, and make you very clear and aware about what the heck your problem is anyhow! I'm sorry! I don't mean to make light of this. Wait, yes I do.

I want you to lighten up and see the process is easier than you think. Sometimes, the process of uncovering what is blocking you from moving forward and expanding is even fun. Often, the process is emotionally moving.

One thing for sure: there is always an experience of relief or release. The eye opening experience changes life as you know it. Your life will become happier, brighter, and better, better and better.

You will finally be able to dispose of the old shit you've been lugging around. In Chapter Two, I alerted you to the unloading process. Unload, and you'll feel loads better.

I recommend two techniques and a program to help change what is stored in your subconscious memory. The first is B.E.S.T., short for Bio Energetic Synchronization Technique.

Dr. M. Ted Morter, Jr. developed this technique almost 40 years ago.

Dr. Morter, practicing as a chiropractor, was told in a dream to never move another bone again. When Dr. Morter went back to his office, he followed the dream instructions. Dr. Morter found he actually had greater success with his patients when he didn't move their bones.

He listened to his inner guidance, Source/Higher Self/ God, and he figured out another way to balance and align his patients without moving bones.

When we sleep, we are connected to our Source. Our dreams can be very enlightening. Sleep is very important in the healing process. Most healing occurs while we are sleeping. Whenever we are closer to Source/God, we feel better.

B.E.S.T. is a gentle non-force technique similar to acupressure. Information is found through the use of muscle testing. *You* are the person being muscle tested. *The essential information comes from you.*

In muscle testing, your arm is stretched out to the side. You are asked to hold a strong muscle after you make a statement. If you are able to hold a strong muscle, the statement is true for you. If your statement is false and doesn't work for you, the muscle strength is weak.

The test is not about a strong muscle. Muscle testing is about testing how quickly the muscle locks in. If your muscle doesn't lock in, you will not be able to hold your arm strong.

Using a chart, the practitioner discovers which of your emotions is triggered through muscle testing. You are given a word raising thoughts, beliefs and feelings/emotions.

Contact points are held by the practitioner, while you are instructed to position your eyes in a certain direction and breathe, or hold a breath. The contacts might be held at the temples, the base of the skull, or above the eyes at your brow. You focus on *how you feel* about whatever comes up with the word with which you are presented, while the practitioner waits for the pulses at each contact to synchronize.

The idea behind the B.E.S.T. technique is to remove the interference and/or distractions which demand the attention of your natural ability to heal every aspect of your life. The most common and most obvious aspect in need of healing is physical illness.

B.E.S.T. is used by practitioners all over the world who practice mind/body healing, and who recognize the body is more than just the sum of its parts.

Many factors affect the body's condition. Emotional issues from the past, as well as choices we are currently making, all affect the balance of our beings.

When we are out of balance, our bodies become exhausted, and pain and/or even disease develop. Everything in our life is affected when we are out of balance.

When we are out of balance, we are further from Love, and not connected to Source. We therefore just don't feel good, in any way, shape or form!

B.E.S.T. balances the body both physically and emotionally. The most common comments after a B.E.S.T. session are "I feel calmer, more centered and focused. I am much clearer on what has been holding me up. I feel hopeful. I can move my neck (or arm, leg etc,.)."

B.E.S.T. technique is very empowering to the client. A cooperative effort is definitely shared between the client and practitioner.

The best aspect of B.E.S.T. is that you are helped to unload what you no longer need. You can become present and focused in the moment, and take control of your life. You can find out more about B.E.S.T. by going to www.morter.com.

Psych-k, founded by Robert Williams, is the other of my top two technique choices. Rob is a psychologist with a prior 14 year business career. Much like Dr. Morter, Rob was guided by God/Source to do the work he is doing now. Actually, Rob was *shown* the work that he does now.

As he describes in his book, *The Missing ~~Piece~~ Peace In Your Life!*, Rob was already frustrated with the typical counseling formula of Insight + Willpower = Change. Rob had several clients that were full of *it (I mean insight)*. His clients perceived how they became unhappy in their lives. However, they were still not experiencing their heart's desires.

One day in December of 1988, Rob was extremely frustrated. He was preparing for a workshop, experiencing financial pressure due to the holidays, and had to take more than one trip to the printer.

Rob got his answers. He could not seem to get the marketing flyer for the workshop right. Every time he thought he had the flyer corrected he discovered another mistake. He finally threw his arms up in exasperation and sat outside in the cold winter air, to literally cool off. With his teeth clenched, he asked out loud, "Okay God, if you don't want me to do what I am doing, what *do* you want me to do?"

He sat in silence. Within minutes, the beginning of what now is called Psych-k expressed itself in his mind. When the information finished being down loaded, he ran to his computer, and wrote the technique now known as Psych-k.

Rob is a perfect example of how the connection to God/Source brings you right into love. Rob loves what he does now. I believe, no, I *know:* when you are connected to Source and you ask a question, you will get the absolute correct answer.

In fact, every answer you get while connected to Source is exactly right. I suggest you ponder or ask your important questions only when connected to Source.

Quiet your mind through meditation or *breathing* (something that we often forget to do), or get angry like Rob did, and ask Source. Wait (it doesn't usually take too long), and you will receive perfect answers and often direction.

True for all of us, as in Rob's experience, anger is a powerful emotion, one which can offer great relief, and often the relief results in an immediate connection to Source. Anger, such as Rob's, is frequently the emotion which moves you in to action.

Psych-k also uses muscle testing to determine the client's priority for healing. The practitioner refers to a number of different charts in order to test different categories.

The healing priority for the client is identified in one of several categories, including self-esteem, relationships, personal power, spirituality, health/body, prosperity and grief/loss.

There are several types of balancing performed with Psych-k. Psych-k is a self-empowering technique used to change beliefs and perceptions keeping you from achieving your full potential.

Bruce Lipton supports and promotes the use of Psych-k, referring to Psych-k in his own book, *The Biology of Belief*. He also conducts seminars regularly with Rob Williams. Dr. Lipton's work focuses on a new understanding, at the cutting edge of science, theorizing about how our perceptions of our environment or our beliefs directly control the activity of our genes.

In other words, our thoughts, attitudes and beliefs create the conditions of our body and our lives, i.e., whether we are healthy or unhealthy, successful or not successful.

Balancing and integrating the left and right sides of the brain, Psych-k changes negative beliefs held in our subconscious mind.

The subconscious mind is like the mainframe computer of the mind. Much more powerful than the conscious mind, the subconscious runs all the programs.

To change the printout of your life, you have to first change the program. In other words, the subconscious has to come into agreement with the conscious mind in order for us to achieve our full potential.

Psych-k changes beliefs at the subconscious level, and lives change and improve dramatically. Your life doesn't have to be predetermined. You can actually have a say in it. To find out more about Psych-k go to www.psych-k.com.

I also belong to a program called AIM (all inclusive method) developed by Stephen Lewis, author of Sanctuary the path to consciousness. AIM is a program in which my family and I have experienced an elevation in our level of consciousness and the result has been clarity and awareness. Personally I have experienced a powerful connection to source and my own healing power since being on the AIM program. Just nine months after joining the AIM program I wrote The Journey from fear to love is shorter than you think. My entire family, including my two dogs, is on the program. Since being on the AIM program we have experienced an abundance of health and energy. You can find out more about the AIM program at their website www.energeticmatrix.com

Where is the ride I promised? Let's look at how B.E.S.T. and Psych-k helped me. B.E.S.T. is the technique that woke me up. I shared with you the nightmare that I had for several years. I use to be terrified during the nightmare. I would wake up in total fear, white as a ghost, with blood curdling screams.

My husband Ben remembers all too well. The insight I gained through the use of B.E.S.T. was the beginning of the end of my nightmare, as well as the beginning of the fantastic ride I've been on for over 20 years.

Waking up is the only way to take the ride. The ride is waiting for you. I believe through techniques like B.E.S.T. or Psych-k, you too can wake up.

I promise you will enjoy an incredible journey and the ride of your life. The bottom line is that what you believe is what will work for you. It doesn't matter what it is, as long as you believe.

Medicine might work for you or natural healing methods may hold the answers you seek. How well any healing technique (natural healing or medicine) works for you depends on what you believe.

You hold the power. Your thoughts and beliefs send messages to your body. Your body basically follows your orders. If you buy into the medical doctors' beliefs and directions, you have signed an unwritten contract. Whatever the doctor says is what you believe.

The same is true if you buy into the fact that **you** have the say about how things are going to go for you. Believe yourself and believe in yourself!

Most people believe exclusively one way or the other. Others have beliefs somewhere in between. What you believe can heal you completely. Or perhaps what you believe, if it is not in your best interest, may just maintain you until you die.

I don't know about you, but I certainly want to be more than maintained until I die. I don't want to be less than the best I can be.

I guess I'll choose door number one and go with what I believe can work with me to become all I already am (perfect, well and wonderful). Go with what you believe, because it is the only thing that will work for *you.*

Once again, you will have to access your feelings in order to perceive what you believe. *You have to believe with feeling for anything to work.*

I guarantee when you fall into Love and out of fear you will believe what *you* believe, with heart felt feeling. Believing is seeing. How lovely: what you see **can** be.

Chapter 7
Does the Journey Ever End? Is the Journey Really Worth It?

No and yes. Of course, my opinion is based on my life and my experiences. We have already established we are *all* very wise and wonderful. If I were you, I might be inclined to believe me and my opinions. I believe me.

I do not believe that the journey ever ends. I do believe that the journey *is* really worth it. In fact, the journey is the most important part of our life experience because the journey is what life is all about.

We all already have a pretty good idea of what the perceived end or destination of our travels will be, but *the journey is what is unfolding right now.*

The journey of life offers great opportunities, and can be a lot of fun. The journey is especially valuable if you leave fear out as much as possible.

The purpose of this book is to help you learn how to live a life free of fear. Some fear is good because fear gives you guidance when you need to pay attention, possibly avoid something or change direction. *Notice, though, that living in fear is not good.*

Some people may find value in a fearful journey. Such fear-invested folks may get pumped up by fear, and may have no interest in learning about living a life with less fear. Perhaps fear is all that is known to people who are fear-invested, who find their comfort zone by living with some fear.

I believe that the journey is a lot more joyful and fun with as little fear involved as possible. The less fear, the happier and healthier you'll be. Being happier and healthier has to be an added perk to the journey, don't you think?

It seems that what most people do on this journey is get stuck doing the same things over and over instead of trying something new. Their focus is on the problem, instead of the solution. People then get more of the problem, and none or less of the solution.

Rob Williams illustrates this point with a story describing a fly trying desperately to escape through a closed window. This fly demonstrates *problem focused* behavior versus *solution focused* behavior. The fly is *trying harder instead of smarter* in the most basic way. The fly spends its energy on useless attempts to fly *through* the window. Even though it makes no progress, the fly continues to try harder and harder.

There is no hope that the fly will survive taking the route it has chosen, and the struggle is part of the problem. Even though there is no way that the fly's attempts will be successful, it continues to *try harder*. The end result of this continued behavior is death. The door, however, is open across the room, and with little effort, the fly could escape to the outside and be free.

Rob asks, "Why doesn't the fly try another approach, something dramatically different?" With the goal of escaping, why would the fly continue until it dies, doing the same thing over and over again to no avail?

Somehow this must be the only thing that makes sense to the fly. Unfortunately, the end result for the fly will be *the end.* Trying harder, doing the same thing with the same dead end result, will not solve the problem at hand.

The problem continues to exist over and over. If the fly would just look in another direction, it would discover an obvious solution.

If you don't change what you are doing, thinking, feeling and/or believing, you'll keep getting more of the same stuff you are already getting.

Albert Einstein defines *"Insanity: doing the same thing over and over again and expecting different results."*

Now my question to you: Do you think that you are smarter than a fly, for crying out loud? After all, flies are attracted to shit, in fact flies live for it.

I am in no way attracted to shit of any kind, and I do not take pleasure in banging my head on a closed window over and over again. How about you?

Since we aren't flies, and we are not on suicide missions, perhaps we should consider finding ways to really make this journey of life worth it.

That isn't to say that everything that you have had happen *for you* up until now hasn't contributed in some way to making the journey worth it. It might have been important for you to hit your head on the window or fall directly into a pile of shit, in order to find out this is not anything you ever want to experience again in this life time.

As you look back (for just a moment) at all of your "negative" experiences, notice how far you have come, what wisdom you have gained, and be grateful and thankful.

If it weren't for some of these not so great times, you would not have the crystal clear concept of what it is you *do want* in your life. You can now pat yourself on the back and appreciate yourself and all that you have accomplished. Have a party just because you are wonderful you.

The important thing is that you continue to realize that in many situations, you have probably had great success when you tried something drastically different.

I never refinanced anything in my life before I refinanced my house. The result was getting my family out of financial hell. If I were a fly, I would have just banged my head against the window and fallen into a pile of shit.

As you come up against new challenges, or what appear to be challenges, please remember that you are incredibly capable and powerful.

I have no doubt that you have demonstrated your fantabulous self on more than one occasion. All you need to do is access a memory of one of those times when you were being fantabulous. By recalling and re-experiencing this memory, you can be empowered again and again and continue to move closer to love and out of fear.

We are not flies, shit does not make us happy and joyful on our journeys, and we do not have to die trying to get to the good stuff!!! We can try smarter, not harder, because we are worthy beings with choices.

The most important choice (in my opinion) is to feel good. If you just keep heading toward feeling better, I know that you will get to wherever it is that you want to go, and the journey will be *so worth it.*

I'm writing this book because it feels sooooo good and it has taken 20 years to get it done. Everything I have done that has helped me to feel better has pointed me in the direction of completing this book.

Notice -- I behaved like the fly for a while, and banged my head and fell into some shit. When I quit the head banging, and tried something dramatically different, everything came together effortlessly.

Well-being abounds for everyone who not only recognizes their well-being is available, but welcomes it with open arms. I think the best part of the journey is the way it unfolds. *If you are in a place of gratitude and joy, things seem to happen effortlessly.*

Every time you are feeling a negative emotion, let the negative emotion be a red flag to you: You are blocking yourself from the joyous journey you are so very worthy of having.

I have so much fun noticing how easy things come to be when I am easy about everything. When I lighten up and let things go, what I want comes easier.

As I start to live in the solution instead of the problem (in this case feeling good about *my being the solution*), the results are no surprise to me. The more I take notice of the joy and happiness in my life, the more happiness and joy show up in my experience.

The law of attraction is always working. I mentioned before -- this is not rocket science.

Just choose whether or not you can allow yourself to be happy and joyful. It is that easy. If you allow happiness and joy, happiness and joy will flow right into your life.

So many of us don't allow happiness to flow to us because we listen to others instructing us about what we can and can not allow in our lives.

If we are really happy, people tend to think that there is either something seriously wrong with us, or we are likely up to no good. To many people, the world is a miserable place. If you're walking around with a smile on your face in the middle of this worldly mess, people invested in misery might wonder what the heck is up with you.

Perhaps, I would guess, a great part of the population would assume that you have a mental condition. In fact you do – the condition diagnosed as obsessive happiness and joy or O.H.J. for short.

Earlier, we considered a flawed view defining rich people, focusing on the notion that the wealthy must be doing something morally incorrect in order to be having so much fun and be so rich. I suspect many people are thinking along the same lines when they see those of us afflicted with O.H.J. Some support groups perpetuate this erroneous view.

Many support organizations/groups are designed to help people feel better about their misery. Somehow, some way, these groups strive to show you that you are a better person for enduring, tolerating, and struggling really hard.

The general view is the harder you work in this life, the more worthy you are of all you have and receive. In the case of the fly, his reward could be presented after he dies on the on the window sill where his lifeless body lies. How did working harder and harder help the fly? Which of us would like to end up dead from taking the same ineffective action, always in vain? After all, this is really all a line of crap we get fed in regard to working harder.

Trying to control conditions, people or anything outside of you makes the journey feel less worth it, because your journey becomes very frustrating and no fun.

We talked about "control issues" in earlier chapters, and I feel it necessary to revisit some of these "control issues" again (sounds like *I* could have a control issue, but it's my book). Your life, my book, are all things over which we each have control. When you try to control anything outside of you, the final outcome is never good or desirable. The final outcome of control just doesn't ever work out well.

The only control you have is over yourself and your actions, reactions and choices. You can not control other people or situations. Focusing on only controlling yourself and your actions/reactions *seems* like it should be easy enough, but sometimes it is really tough to only focus on what you do have control over: you and you alone. Are you bored? Make *yourself* more interesting.

Control issues are especially evident when we think about family and close friends. As a parent, I really think sometimes that life would be so much easier if my children would just do exactly as I direct.

After all, I know more than they do, don't I? Actually, I don't! How could I possibly know more about their *personal* journeys? As we previously discussed, parents can and should guide children, and we can and should be open to receiving guidance in *return from* our children.

Our kids are very wise, and their perspectives about life are less contaminated than ours. Therefore, our children's view of life more closely resembles what ours would be if we were wearing the rose colored glasses discussed in Chapter Six. Our children know more about what *they* should or should not be doing than we, their parents, do.

Don't throw *Fear to Love* down quite yet. I do have a point. Even with our children, we truly have limited control, and ultimately the decisions about leading their own lives belong to them.

Sure, we can control where they live while they live with us (usually) and what they eat (to some extent), but they will always find a way to be who they are.

Children are very creative and will find a way to get what they want. Kids can get junk food at a friend's house, for example, or feed the dog under the table. Children can frequently find ways to be other places if they would rather be living somewhere else.

I am not saying you should throw in the towel as a parent. I just suggest you do what you *feel* is right as a parent. Know that regardless of all of your efforts, children will always be trying to do what they *feel* is right for their own journey.

Encourage your children to use their own internal guidance or intuition. When your children are ready to leave your home, their intuitive abilities will be enhanced instead of squashed.

The more you allow your children to be who they are by giving them room to express themselves, the happier you and your children will be. When children have less to push against, they tend to be easier to live with and to raise.

I am not suggesting that you allow your children to mistreat or abuse you as a parent. Your children live in *your* home, where there should be mutual respect. I feel that you have the right to set certain rules.

Just don't *over-rule* to the point that your children become powerless and have a harder time figuring out who they are. You won't be doing your kids any favors. You could potentially end up with your 40 year old adult child still living at home because he or she was not allowed to become their own person. Children of controlling parents might become very dependent on what their parents think and feel, because they haven't learned how to think and feel for themselves.

If this happens, I'm sorry, but you *will* have to take the blame for creating your own circumstances. Even as a fellow parent, I don't know how to get you off the hook for this one. The old saying "You've created a monster" applies here.

When you give a kid less room to be themselves, you also give your children more reasons to push against everything. Our children are on their own journeys, and we really have no idea what their journeys are going to be.

Each individual's journey is very personal. The best course of action for parents is to provide a loving environment and room for children to grow. By *room*, I mean give your children their space to be who they are.

It is also important to your children to know they have your blessings to be who they are. Let your children know you love and care for them! Let your children know what you want most for them is their own happiness, joy, love and well-being.

Also let your children know that you are aware of their own insight into their lives. We all have the same gift of knowingness because we all can *feel* what feels good or bad.

Teach your children to tap into their internal wisdom and trust: they can and will do just that. Reminding children of their innate ability to *know* empowers them. Don't forget to also let your children know that they are worthy of the best life they could ever imagine.

I focus on children because I am a parent. I do feel that the subject of raising children provides several examples of how you can quickly make your journey miserable, or not miserable.

We once were all children. Even if you are not raising kids, you can think back and remember how you felt as a child. You might be able to see how you were empowered or not empowered. Regardless of your previous experience, you are *now* empowered, so have fun.

Let us move on to the subject of whether the journey ever ends or not. The length of the journey is something not everyone agrees upon. The amount of time which the journey lasts can be a spooky topic for a lot of people.

My opinion on the length and continuation of the journey is very much just *my opinion*. I wish to explain, the best way I can, about my personal experiences which caused me to form my current opinion. Turn on the lights. We might get a little spooky.

Fourteen years ago my father in-law died very suddenly in an accident while out of the country. He was only 55 years old. We were all horribly shocked, to say the least. My husband had a very difficult time accepting the death of his father.

My father in-law and I shared a special bond. We connected well, and in a lot of ways, he filled some gaps in my life my own father was never able to fill.

The combination of my two Dads was a wonderful balance for me personally. Now both Dads are gone, and I do miss them. I have, however, felt their presence in my life several times since they have moved on.

I say moved on because I feel that there is really no such thing as death. Thus the journey never ends. I have no scientific evidence to back this up. I do have a *feeling* in my gut, and personal experiences have drawn me to this conclusion.

This book is all about basing your life on how you *feel*. I feel and believe we were spiritual beings before we ever became physical beings. I've felt this since my childhood. Let me share my logic.

If we were spiritual beings first, then it only makes sense to me that in the "end", after we (pass away) or move on, we return to our state of spiritual being. Actually, our spiritual aspect is never truly separated from who we are in this physical life. As human beings in this physical life, we often (erroneously) feel and think that we are separated from our spiritual selves.

I believe that after we leave this physical body, we become purely spiritual again. Since spirits don't die, the only conclusion I can draw is that we don't die either, because our spirit is the true core of who we are. Therefore, the journey never ends.

I have personally had several experiences that make me believe our spirit lives on after we die. After my father in-law died, I had several very vivid dreams in which I could see him and hear him.

In these dreams, he wore the same shirt, which I had given him for Christmas, every time. He was trying to talk to my husband Ben, but Ben wasn't listening.

Dad expressed his frustration with Ben's lack of listening each time he came to me in these dreams. My father-in-law wanted to let my husband Ben know that he (my father-in-law) was okay and all was well. I know it sounds like "just a dream", but I have had lots of these kinds of "dreams" after loved ones have moved on.

My vivid dream connecting me to my paternal grandmother finally convinced me that I had some real contact with the spirit of a loved one who passed on.

I awoke from what seemed like an all night long visit with my Grandmother. In this "dream", she sat with me at my piano (she played by ear when she was alive) and played, and talked to me all night.

She told me a lot. I had only seen my grandmother a few times when I was very young. She died by the time I was nine. The morning after my dream, I called my father as soon as I awoke because I had to tell him about this extraordinary visit.

I was able to describe my grandmother's physical appearance in detail even though before this "dream" I had no memory of what she looked like. I was also able to tell my Dad the details of our conversation.

I shared one particular very private piece of information with my dad, given to me by my grandmother in the dream. He was amazed. He told me that there was no way that I would know about that particular experience, unless his mother had told me. He had never shared the information with anyone.

As I held the phone, I could hear my mother in the background, standing near dad, asking "Why didn't you ever tell me that?" "*I've* never told anyone," my dad replied. He said the hair on his arms was standing up.

He then told me that my grandmother was calling for me on her death bed (I never knew). I was her only granddaughter.

After my father passed on, I had "dreams" about him, too. As I have already shared with you, in one dream he was painting and enjoying himself immensely. He never painted when he was physically here.

Dad expressed a happy and peaceful calm in his demeanor. I know this doesn't sound especially convincing. Since my dad has been gone (about a year and a half now), I have felt his presence spiritually.

I felt dad's presence very strongly at his memorial service. My youngest son Alex, who was 10 at the time, decided that he was going to speak, and share some nice things about his grandpa. When he got up there, he couldn't speak.

I waited for his dad to go up and save Alex. When I realized that wasn't going to happen, I went up and stood with my son. The church was full with about 200 people (my dad was well liked).

I took the microphone, and spoke to buy my son some time. I reminisced about my dad and talked about the ways that his children and grandchildren were like him. I even joked about some experiences we shared together.

People were laughing and smiling. I think that the memorial service took a turn away from the energies of sadness, and became more of a celebration of my dad's life. Everyone who spoke after me told funny or loving stories about my dad. (People commented afterwards about how much they enjoyed what I shared about dad, and that their experience at my dad's memorial service made it the nicest memorial service they had ever attended.)

I also reminded everyone that dad would always be with us spiritually, and shared that I could feel his presence with us. Suddenly, as I was speaking, I realized how many people were looking at me. I usually have stage fright.

I get very nervous, my throat dries up on me, and I feel as if I can't breathe. I could see the audience in the church really well, and to my amazement, I was still able to continue talking.

Something, in those moments, was very different. At first, I wanted to get off the stage for a moment because I fully expected to lose my breath and have my throat dry up (as usual) any second.

At the very moment in which I wanted to leave the stage, I felt as if someone had their arms around both my son and me. I heard a voice encourage me to continue. I knew the voice had to be my dad.

My son spoke next -- he was so sweet and genuine about his love for his grandfather. Alex also said I was like my dad.

After the whole thing was over, my husband said, "Wow! You did great! You held that microphone as if you had done it a thousand times."

The truth is, I had never in my life used a microphone before and had no recollection of just having held one. I know that my dad was with us spiritually, guiding me, and I also know that he loved every bit of it, because he enjoyed talking about himself. (I mean in a good way.) Dad had lots of stories he liked to tell. I believe all of us, sharing together at the memorial service, with a little help from dad, accomplished the telling of some of our favorite stories about Dad.

My most recent spiritual experience also had to do with my father. Since my dad has been gone, I have had a few times where I have been trying to figure out how to handle some of life's little bumps, and I find myself asking my dad.

Whenever I ask dad, I feel that I will receive an incredibly insightful answer. The answers I have received from dad have also proven to be perfect solutions, or at least headed me in a better direction, toward love instead of fear.

One day, not long ago, I asked dad a question and I received an answer. I decided to ask more questions, and guess what? I got more answers.

I felt a little freaked out, so I asked "How long can I talk to you?" The answer: "As long as you want, I'm always here."

Okay! At this point, I was sitting on the floor crying. Then I heard, "Why are you crying?" I answered, "Because I miss you."

Again I was told, "I am always here." At this point, I was writing things down, because dad had my undivided attention. My dad also told me to underline this statement. I asked about 30 minutes worth of questions, and received answers for every single one!

At one point, I asked if I could have a sign that I wasn't crazy. I asked if I could feel his hug, and I did. I felt as though dad had his arms around me, and I was leaning into his arms with my left shoulder.

I experienced much more that afternoon, but I offer you the clincher making me believe, in no uncertain terms, that my father was with me in spirit in a very real way.

I went down stairs, and my husband Ben stopped me, asking if I had just had a B.E.S.T. adjustment. He said I looked a little zoned. I could only respond by explaining, "Well kind of, do you want to hear about it?"

I then told my entire family what had just taken place. Ben and my children all thought my encounter with dad was very cool.

When I told my husband what dad had said about him, Ben was brought to tears. Ben's were not tears of sadness. He also felt dad's spiritual presence.

Here is what captured everyone's attention. My oldest son Steven gave me a hug, burying his head into my left shoulder. Steven was telling me how cool he thought my entire experience was, when all of a sudden, he pulled back from me, and appeared to be kind of startled.

"You smell like grandpa," my son said excitedly. My heart leaped as I recalled my dad's distinctive fragrance—the smell of Old Spice after shave, and his clothes which carried the scent of his closet in the old house.

"What?" I said.

Steven repeated, "You smell like grandpa."

I asked my oldest daughter, Samantha, to come close to me and see if she could catch a scent of grandpa.

"You do smell like grandpa," she agreed.

Next, I asked my husband to do the same. "I don't remember exactly what your dad smelled like," Ben responded, "but you don't smell like you."

"My dad hugged me, he hugged me," I informed my family. All very exciting, and not the least bit spooky.

I have had many other similar experiences in my life, bringing me to the conclusion that the journey never ends.

Every time I've felt the presence of someone who has passed, their presence has felt the same as an angel's presence. Spiritual forms and angels are the same to me. Most people have no problem believing in angels. If you would rather think of the continuous journey as one of keeping company with angels, go ahead.

We all become angelic when we pass on sounds perfectly reasonable to me, and wonderfully beautiful. If you look back at some of your own experiences after a loved one has passed, you too can probably see that you have had similar encounters.

These experiences of ours are all, in my opinion, indications or signs that our journey never ends. The beauty in knowing this journey never ends is that you can take joy in knowing you have plenty of time to get it right.

The better news is that you can't get it wrong, because in the end (what end?) of your physical life, you will with no doubt get the journey right (whether, in this moment, you think you can or not).

The journey is more fun if you work toward *getting it* while you're still here. You have the opportunity to have a fantabulous life, knowing that later will be wonderful too.

Your awareness should help to erase one of the biggest fears people have, which is death. There is no sense in fearing something that doesn't exist anyway, is there?

I think while I'm here, I will opt for the full package of happiness, joy, love and fun. While I'm at it, I think I will upgrade to first class. I am making the ride as comfortable as possible. *Come fly with me.*

Chapter 8
Are You Ready for the Ride?

Let's review all of the ways in which you will know if you are ready for the ride. Keep in mind--the journey is the most important part of the ride.

The more prepared you are for the journey, the better the ride will be. If you are well prepared, the ride will go smooth and easy. Think of this process as tuning up your car before a long trip. Check your tires, put gas in the car, check the brakes, change the oil, and check your windshield wipers, because you want to make sure you have perfectly clear visibility.

You wouldn't want to miss anything, and a clear view will help to ensure you don't. I'm telling you: the ride will be beautiful and you will want to absorb it all.

Wear a seat belt, because the ride can be very fast. If you make a wrong turn, you will want to turn around as quick as you can to avoid wasting gas/energy unnecessarily.

Isn't it interesting? We seem to take better care of our cars than we do ourselves! When it comes to us, we let ourselves get overwhelmed, or wait for a crisis to hit before we are forced to stop and look at what is going on.

Maybe you should treat yourself as well as you treat your car. Stop and check in every so often to see how your energy is running. Check to see if your gas tank is on empty, or close to it.

Every once in a while a tune up would be a good idea. Use something like B.E.S.T. or Psych-k and get a good massage or just stop and breathe in and out and appreciate each breath.

Now that you have checked under the hood (so to speak), the next really important thing to do is to have passion for the ride you are about to take. It is similar to the passion you feel for a vacation into which you have put a lot of time and energy planning.

The difference -- this life journey is *the journey of a life time* (your life, that is), and includes every vacation that you will ever take and much more. I want to make sure you are really ready for the happiness, joy, love and fun which are there for you, just waiting for you to grab hold of and free fall right into these joyous gifts!

Your free fall into joy and love will be especially true for you when you decide **you are worthy** of it. Once you get all of your fears out of the way and learn how to quickly dispose of any new ones as they show up, the journey unfolds quickly and effortlessly. By this point in the book, you have already recognized the progress you have made toward love and away from fear. Take a moment. Pat yourself on the back!

First things first -- if you have figured out some ways you have gotten into fear, you are starting to become aware and awake. Being awake for this ride is pretty important, because if you aren't awake, you will miss all the good stuff.

Also, by understanding how you have gotten into fear, you will start to come up with ways to get out and start moving towards love.

If you don't even know what the problem is, how can you possibly solve it? The next step is to be okay with where you are right now and to be accountable for getting yourself into your current position.

You have to be able to own the journey you have taken so you can feel empowered to change the direction in which your journey is going. If you can create your journey, then you can recreate your journey just as well. Start paying attention to which wolf you are feeding.

Remember and don't ever forget how worthy and wonderful you are and have always been. This awareness of your worth is a priority in order to be sure you are ready for the ride.

Understanding the law of attraction *(what you put out is what you get back)* will help you immensely along the way on this ride. Understanding that the law of attraction is always working will cause you to become more accountable for your life. You won't be able to blame anyone else when you truly grasp how the law of attraction works.

You will see how you have gotten what you've gotten. Soon, you will decide you want things to be different in some areas of your life.

You have probably attracted several things and experiences into you life with which you are very happy. When you realize what these are, and look at how *your* thoughts and actions brought them to you, you will have vital information.

This information will help you to continue to bring into your life more of what you want, and less of what you don't wat.

The combination of practice and celebrating the results will inspire you to have the best life you can have.

As you elevate your life through conscious behavior, you will become an artist and your life will look beautiful. Seeing the good in everything and everyone will be easy for you. Soon it will seem ridiculous to you to live any other way. *It's all good.*

Liking and loving yourself is essential because your approval and love for *yourself* is most important. You spend the most time with yourself. For your sake, wouldn't it be nice if you loved your own company?

Recognize your own greatness and let yourself shine. *Offering and allowing your own radiance is a wonderful way to give to others, because as you shine, you give others permission to shine as well.*

Other people follow your lead. Also, remember you can do great things while you are here in physical form. Do not underestimate your greatness. Only when you decide you can't do something does it becomes true. As Henry Ford said *"If you think you can OR if you think you can't, you will ALWAYS be right."*

Think about this equation. Awake = clarity = power = movement = change. Life is movement and change, with never a dull moment.

You get to choose how things go for you. Even as I write this book, or say out loud over and over what I am writing, I feel uplifted and empowered. I am reminded of how great we all are, and I feel warm and wonderful all over. There is nothing that can bring me down except for me. Most often, I just don't go there anymore. Nor should you!

Treating yourself like you treat your best friend will help you to be in the perfect place to make really nice choices. You want only the best for a best friend, don't you?

Taking time to appreciate *you* will enhance the ride, because you will *feel* like you deserve the best that life has to offer. Take time every day to have some quiet time so you can tune into your Source/God. You will then be able to pinpoint better what you desire in your life.

Be grateful and thankful for all you already have, and your heart's desires will come easier because you won't be blocking your gratitude with negative feelings.

Negative feelings can keep you right where you are, recreating over and over exactly what you have and nothing new. Life as it is can't change until you change how you look at your life and how you *feel* about your life.

After you change how you feel about your life, your actions will change. The goal for this ride should be to enjoy life as much as possible. Acknowledging your feelings is the first step in changing your thoughts. When you change your thoughts into more positive thoughts, you will feel better instantly.

The root cause of almost every problem seems to be the feeling of unworthiness. You feel unworthy because you are not connected to your Source/God or Higher Self. You are not connected because you don't feel worthy. It is a vicious cycle.

The lack of connection had to come first in our physical life, because we were already connected before we ever arrived here. As you are more and more deeply connected, you will remember you have always been worthy. This awareness of your own worthiness solves problems quickly.

You look at everything different and not much is seen as a problem. What is perceived as a problem won't last long.

You are just too worthy to let anything become an issue. Some will see you as a little big headed for feeling so sure *all is always well.* It is okay-- other people just haven't figured out *all is well* yet and you really do know better.

Since you are now paying attention to where you put your attention, you have tapped into your personal power to change your life. You know where ever you focus your attention will expand and get bigger and bigger.

Ask yourself: what do I want to expand in my life? Watch what you want to expand grow, and celebrate the power of you! You have the power to change what or how you are thinking, or to simply choose not to believe what you are thinking.

Two bumper stickers I saw relate here. The first one said "Don't believe everything you think." At this point you know when you don't feel good you need stop to think about what you are thinking about (examine your thoughts), and don't always believe your thoughts.

The second bumper sticker said "Change is inevitable, growth is optional." Now you know it is your choice whether or not you are going to grow with the changes which naturally occur with life, or if you are going to stunt your growth because you can't see how everything happens *for you, not to you.*

Remember to stop and ask the question "*What the for?*" *Everything happens for you not to you.* This awareness and understanding will help you to see there is always the potential to grow and reach a higher level of functioning.

Moving towards love through growth is always more fun than turning toward fear where everything is pretty well dead. *Things grow where there is love and die where there is fear.*

Dr. Emoto writes in his book, *The Hidden Messages In Water,* about an experiment done with rice. Hundreds of families conducted this rice experiment, with identical results.

Rice was put in two glass jars and everyday for a month the family conducting the experiment said "thank you" to one jar of rice and "you fool" to the other jar.

After a month, the rice which received the "thank you" messages from the family started to ferment, while the rice which received the "you fool" messages rotted and turned black very quickly.

A third jar of rice was added and just ignored. The results: the ignored jar of rice rotted even faster than the "you fool".

It seems the idea is true: some attention, even if the attention is negative, is better than no attention.

Like the Alabama song says, *"Oh, I believe there are angels among us."* When you are truly connected to God/Source or Higher Self, you know you are always being watched over. In times of crisis or sorrow, if you have paid attention, you have felt the presence of someone watching over you.

If you are connected to Source you will feel loved, because God is love. *It is impossible to be connected to God and experience fear simultaneously.* By now, you realize the result of getting wrapped up in our personal dramas is distraction, which causes to us to be unable to hear God.

Our dramas are fear-based. While in the midst of our dramas, we just can't hear over our own noise. You can quiet your mind through meditation, yoga, exercise or *just breathe, for crying out loud.*

By now, as you have probably figured out, lack of oxygen will slow down your progress on your journey. The best thing to do to quiet your mind is to focus on everything for which you are grateful and thankful.

The attitude of gratitude is more actively productive than meditation, because you are consciously participating in your life, and making progress at the same time.

We already know after you die in this physical world, the continued journey will be *fantabulous.* While you are here on this planet, you can tune into your Source, creating a fantabulous journey here and now.

Your God or Source is your Higher Self, and God is always tuned into you. Are you tuned in and listening to God/Source? You know whether or not you are tuned in by how you feel.

Focusing in on how you are feeling makes it easier for you to turn towards love more quickly, because you are now alert to being overtaken by fear.

Being grateful and thankful as often as possible will help you to continue on the path towards love. Being grateful and thankful will help to quiet your mind so you can hear over your own noise.

Also, as you know, only when you can be okay with your current situation, then and only then, will you be able to move towards all the other places you want to be.

Send love out and you will get love back. Another perk with connection to God/Source: since you are not living in fear, you can accomplish anything.

By now, you understand you have to slow down enough to connect to your Source. As you spend some time being grateful, more experiences, things and people to be grateful and thankful for will effortlessly flow into your life.

Now you understand how your feelings can guide you towards love, or not. You also understand how holding on to feelings like anger and resentment is like taking poison.

These emotions are toxic and damage the person who is feeling them, not the person towards whom they are directed. If you feel anger and resentment towards another, you are the one who suffers. You are creating a form of self abuse.

Seek better feelings, so you can stop creating the toxic energy which comes with poisonous feelings. Find an anchoring thought or carry a gratitude stone.

One of the most helpful things you can allow into your life is forgiveness. If you truly forgive, an interfering issue can be let go of and you can move towards love once again.

With forgiveness comes freedom. You free yourself. Most of us create our own prisons, and we don't realize we alone hold the key to our freedom. I think *you* get this by now.

As Dr. Emoto's research demonstrates, we are made up of mostly water. The saying "go with the flow" takes on a whole new meaning when you realize *you are the flow.*

The natural flow of well being really does lie within you. Also, if you remember, Dr. Emoto says every individual vibrates energetically at 570 trillion times a second.

We are incredibly powerful. This explains why prayer is so effective. Multiply 570 trillion times per second times, let's say, 100 people praying for the same thing, you can imagine the power of this particular prayer.

You alone, praying for yourself, are incredibly powerful. We need to pray correctly for the prayer to be answered, according to our heart's desire.

Remember, the law of attraction works with prayer as well as anything else. Pray as if you have already received what you are praying for. If you pray from a place of fear you will attract more of that which you fear.

For example, praying for an illness to "please go away" is more in fear than saying "thank you for my healthy body". When my husband is out of town, the prayer I share with my children goes like this: "Thank you for dad being safe and for him coming home safely."

According to Dr. Emoto, "thank you" creates beautiful and complete crystals. This means the vibration of "thank you" energetically is powerfully positive. If you pray with thankfulness, the result will also be powerful and positive -- the only possible outcome from a thankful place.

Remember what we have discussed about being in a place of thankfulness and gratitude. Thankfulness and gratitude are the only way to get to where you want to be. *How you perceive is what you'll receive.*

If you are truly connected to Source, it is easy to be grateful and thankful. If you are not yet connected to Source, you can connect through an attitude of gratitude and thankfulness.

Slow down, you're going too fast. Spending time in gratitude and thankfulness will help you to slow down. If you don't slow down, you can't figure out what it is that you want in your life. Before you know it, you're dead.

We can't hear over our own noise when we are going too fast. Often, as a consequence, we get hurt. When you're spinning out of control, you run into things. The faster you are going, the more it hurts.

Ask yourself these questions: "Am I doing what makes me happy, what I am passionate about? Or, am I just playing "the game"? (The game is doing what others want or expect us to do rather than what we want to do.)

Do what makes your heart sing and makes your face contort into the shape often referred to as a smile. Like the song from the 80's goes "Don't Worry, Be Happy".

Remember "be, do and have" and you will have everything you truly desire. Be what it is that you want your life to reflect. Just by deciding to truly "be happy", everything you do will reflect the state of being happy, and naturally following, you will have everything you desire in your life.

You are the only director of your life. You don't owe anyone an explanation and the reverse is true for everyone else. Live your truth and stop getting in your own way. People who are truly happy and joyful (from the inside out) usually have all they want in their lives. People are not happy because they have all that they want. Quite the reverse. People have all they want because they are filled with joy and gratitude. Each of our desires and dreams are unique to each of us. Your life is a reflection of your individual wants and desires. *Happiness is relative.*

The most important thing happy people have is happiness and joy. Hopefully, you are starting to, or better yet, you completely get this idea and principle by now.

You will know if you are on the right track by how you are feeling. Good feelings are a good indication that you're on track. Of course, bad feelings mean you need to pay attention and turn toward love. *You do have the power to change the direction in which you are heading.*

What do you expect? By now, you understand your expectations play a huge part in how you are directing your life.

If you expect things to go badly, then things will go badly. If you expect to be successful, then you will be successful.

Expectations can be restricting, and take the joy out of life. Expectations can also be expansive and bring more joy into one's life.

Often, those of us who have great expectations are considered to be arrogant for having great expectations. I can live with that. How about you?

When I expect something, feel it and imagine it, it always happens for me. *Sometimes what happens for me doesn't look exactly the way I expected, but if I look real close I can see I got what I wanted.*

For example, when my husband left his last place of employment after 20 years with the company, his departure was not a want or desire we had placed into the universe.

The desire we very specifically put out together was for Ben to travel significantly less for work, and a desire for financial freedom and independence. The result: Ben left his last job and took a nice severance package with him. He no longer travels for a company.

Ben took a new job where he is able to be home with his family every night. I can more easily finish this book and go on to write my next two books, planned to be published in the near future.

I am always reminded of the fact: I am in control of my life and I am incredibly powerful.

Most people get stuck when it comes to allowing their expectation to manifest. They start to think and do things which sabotage their expectations. They might say things like "Who am I to think I deserve that?", or they stop their actions which were moving them in the direction of their expectation.

I stopped writing for a short time, when I got to the last two chapters of this book. I started to sabotage my success by deciding there is not time for "me" to finish anything.

My children were on summer vacation, and my husband decided to leave his job of 20 years and take a job in another state. He is traveling while I'm finishing this book.

It also looks like we'll be moving very soon. So, what is my problem? I'm letting a little chaos, I mean a little "*life experience*", stop me from my original expectation of completing this book.

After all, everything in my life is created by me. The same is true for you. Oh sure, I could use all of the above as an excuse for getting off track, or I could decide to stick to my expectations.

If I stop and look at it all, everything is going according to the plans Ben and I made. As I shared, it may look different then we expected, but we got what we wanted.

We wanted him to stop traveling for work and for us to become financially free. The job Ben is taking requires very little travel and the opportunities for advancement are great.

We wanted more family time. His current job ends while the kids are on summer break. He will be home *every* night when he takes this new job. Yes, *every* night.

What is the saying? "Be careful what you wish for." I'm only kidding,… *I think.* We love to travel together and want to travel more. This job will take us somewhere we have never lived before, which will give us the ability to travel to local places we have never been before.

My natural tendency is to go upward when others would take a nose dive and crash and burn. *With change comes opportunity, and life is movement and change. Life is opportunity.*

The fact that there are changes happening in my life right now can be used to put a fire under my butt to finish what I've been putting off. The progress I am now making *since the fire*, also shows me that I was using the kids on summer break (along with everything else currently going on) as an *excuse* to fall into my little pity party and decide, "There just isn't time for me".

When I slow down and look a little closer, I can see the good in everything happening *for me* right now.

Since you get this director and expectation stuff, get yourself present and focused in the moment, and get a picture of what you want your life to look like.

If you are happy with the way your life is, then what else do you want or want to do with your life? Whatever you do, the most important thing is to have fun doing it.

"The force is with you." As George Lucas stated, "*Ultimately the force is the larger mystery of the universe. Trusting your feelings is your way into that.*"

If you are feeling bad or having negative feelings, you are heading in the direction of fear and further away from love. Sometimes these negative feelings will toss you around like a ping pong ball for a while, and it will be more difficult to move towards love.

Don't fight the feeling! Instead, allow it, and work through it, perhaps by allowing forgiveness. As Jesus said *"Forgive them for they know not what they do"*. Jesus practiced forgiveness regularly. Since it worked for him, I will follow His example.

The important thing for you is to learn how to move yourself out bad feelings and towards love, sooner than later. Being in a place of joy as often as possible is an admirable goal.

It is perfectly fine if the path away from fear and towards love is smooth and easy. Suffering is an unnecessary option! Others will disagree with my view, but by now, you don't care what others think.

It is your life and it should be *about how you feel,* don't you think? If you are focused on what other people think, you are wasting valuable time and energy better used on behalf of your life and your desires.

It is okay to look at people who seem be getting everything you would like to have in your life, as an example of what actions you might take. You might not want to do **everything** they are doing.

If someone else has what you want, check out the other persons methods and actions —you might learn something valuable.

You can pick and choose what you desire to bring into your own life. For example, if you look at someone whose life looks the way you would like to have yours look, you might find out he or she has an attitude of gratitude and thankfulness.

Do you have an attitude of gratitude and thankfulness? If not, you might want to consider practicing gratitude and thankfulness in your life, too. See what happens.

You can also look at people who have exactly the opposite of what you want in your life, and use their example to be aware of what you *don't* want.

For example, you might notice someone who is living a life which you do not desire is always complaining or worrying. If you recognize similar behaviors and attitudes in your own life, you may rethink what you are doing and saying.

When the behavior or attitude is the same or similar, positive or negative, then it shouldn't be a big surprise if the outcome is the same or similar.

As you start to realize the power does really lie within you to choose how you want your life to be, you become empowered. With empowerment comes freedom.

You are free to choose the life you want. Learning how to direct your thoughts, by paying attention to how you are feeling, is essential to obtaining personal freedom and power.

As George Lucas tells us, "You've got to trust your feelings" in order to access *"The Force"* within all of us. As you go through different feelings and emotions, let the internal, intuitive part of you lead you naturally up and out of fear, towards love and joy.

You will start to always have your goal of living in joy and love in the forefront of your mind.

You will become like the six million dollar man, and be built better, faster, and stronger than ever before with an outstanding ability to move right back into joy and love.

You won't be faking it; you will use the tools you now have to help you remember love is really what life is all about. It is okay to feel loving, joyful and happy. Feeling these feelings is beyond okay -- feeling loving, joyful and happy is the only thing which makes perfect sense.

Believing is seeing. Children believe and because they do, children get a lot of what they want. If adults would stop to pay attention to how children live their lives when uninterrupted, we would be truly educated.

If you could *believe,* then you would soon *see* also. You have to feel worthy. Generally, children feel worthy. Children believe and have no doubt that Santa and the tooth fairy will come to their house.

Children believe, and through their belief they manifest all kinds of things into their lives. Children enjoy a rich fantasy/daydream life. Children don't spend a lot of time thinking about what they are thinking about. Children just be, do and have.

Children are happy, and dream or imagine what they want. Children do things (without conscious thought) *bringing* them what they have.

For example, when I wanted a pair of shoes as a child, I looked at pictures and at my friend's shoes which looked like the shoes I wanted.

I spent time day dreaming about wearing those shoes to school and how cool I would look. Then my Mom and I went shopping and miraculously I got the shoes I wanted. Or not so miraculously, as I see it now.

My Mom didn't even know I wanted those particular shoes, and I never had to ask her for them. You can do the same thing with adult stuff too.

Remember the story about how we sold our house in Arizona? I believed with all of my heart I would sell my house for over $500,000 even when everyone around me thought I wasn't being realistic. I remember believing it and feeling it so much that I saw it happen in my mind. The sale of my house for over $500,000 became a reality. Good thing I didn't let others reality affect my reality.

Does the journey ever end and is it really worth it? Please recall my opinion: The journey never ends, and yes, the journey is worth it.

We already have a pretty good idea of what the perceived end or destination will be, but the journey is unfolding right now, in this moment.

The journey is especially worth it if you leave fear out as much as possible. To some people, a fearful journey may be worth it because strong negative emotions get them pumped and moving, even if in the direction of fear.

People often function in fear because fear is all they know, and it feels familiar and comfortable to them. It isn't easy to move out of your comfort zone.

The less fear, the happier and healthier you'll be. Being happier and healthier has to be an added perk to the journey, don't you think?

Remember the story about the fly? The fly demonstrates problem focused behavior verses solution focused behavior, trying harder instead of smarter in the most basic way.

Problem focused behavior definitely makes the journey feel like it is not worth it. Trying something dramatically different can turn the journey all the way around and back in the direction of love. We are smarter than flies, so I think we are all capable of figuring out what it is we could try differently.

Sometimes simply doing the exact opposite of what you are currently doing works beautifully. For example, let's say you have a relationship with someone who ridicules you frequently. Do you respond a certain way when they ridicule you? If so, then next time try not reacting or responding at all and see what happens.

It is very likely the ridicule will stop all together. Your response provided the payoff for the person doing the ridiculing. If the ridiculer isn't getting the payoff response anymore, why would he bother to perform the behavior?

Sounds a lot like the advice parents receive when raising children. I guess we are all still children at heart. "Only give your attention to the behavior you are wanting and ignore all the rest", parents are advised. The advice works for everyone.

If you look at some things which have happened in your life, you will probably be able to recall a time or two when you tried something drastically different resulting in great success. I had never refinanced anything before I refinanced my house, and the result was getting my family out of financial hell.

I think that the best part of the journey is the way the journey unfolds. If you are in a place of thankfulness, gratitude and joy, things seem to happen effortlessly.

If you allow happiness and joy, happiness and joy will flow right into your life. Many people don't allow happiness to flow to them because they let others tell them what they can allow or not allow in their lives.

To many people the world is a miserable place. So, if in the middle of this messed up place you are happy, a large number of people will more than likely suspect there is something wrong with you. Perhaps you have the mental condition called O.H.J., short for obsessive happiness and joy. I guess those who don't feel so good and aren't having such a good time, feel better in assuming those who *are happy and joyful* must have something wrong with them, or at least be doing something wrong.

We considered organizations and support groups designed to make miserable people feel better about being miserable. Great news isn't it? These groups somehow, some way, tell you that you are a better person for enduring, tolerating, and struggling really hard. Just remember, **you are smarter than a fly.**

Trying to control anything outside of you also makes the journey feel less worth it because lack of control is very frustrating and no fun. You cannot control situations, and certainly not people. The only thing you can control is you and your actions, reactions and choices.

Sounds easy enough, but sometimes it is really tough to focus on the only thing you do have control over, *you*. This truth is shown to us over and over by children. Children are on their own journeys.

If you try to control children, they will push right back. Pushing back is naturally what any one of us will do if there is an attempt to control our lives.

If children are encouraged, they will use their feelings or intuition as a natural guide. Children are still close enough to love. It makes perfect sense to children to use their own natural ability as a guide, when allowed.

We all have the same gift of knowingness because we all can *feel* what feels good or bad. Children just haven't forgotten as much as adults have. As I have said before, children can teach adults a lot.

We should remind our children they are worthy of the best life they could ever imagine. If we just observe children, they *teach us* worthiness with ease and grace. The way they live their lives is with a natural attitude of worth.

In my opinion, the journey never ends. I've shared several reasons why I hold this personal belief. Many people believe the journey doesn't end due to their religious teachings. If that is why you believe in a never ending journey, Alleluia and Amen!

It doesn't matter why you believe the journey doesn't end. It matters more that you do. I believe we were spiritual beings before we ever became physical beings. I have felt this since I was a child. Children are very wise. If we are spiritual first, it makes sense to me we return to a spiritual state of being.

The beauty in knowing the journey never ends is you can celebrate the fact you have plenty of time to get the journey right. The better news is you can't get it wrong because in the end (what end?) of this physical life, you will, with no doubt, be in pure positive love, whether you think you can now or not.

It is more fun if you can *get to love* or at least lean in that direction while you are still here, because you can have a blast now while knowing you will do the same later. The phrase "heaven on earth" is referring to finding Joy/Love in every earth bound moment.

The idea of your everlasting spiritual being-ness should help to eliminate one of the biggest fears people have, which is death. There is no sense in fearing something that doesn't exist anyway, is there? While we are all here, I think we should opt for the full package of happiness, abundance, joy, love and fun. Here's to Now and Later.

Chapter 9
Let Go and Enjoy the Ride

The way out of the maze is not difficult. In fact, there are several paths out.

When you are in total fear, the path is blurred, blocked or completely invisible to you. Observe my past, as an example.

When I experienced my nightmare, I experienced a state of total fear. I was so consumed by my own fear, that which ever path of escape I attempted led me right back to the terrible fear.

Whenever I headed in the right direction away from fear, fear would take over, I would back track, and fall right into fear once again. I now know that the path out of fear was right in front of me the whole time.

When I started to live closer *to love* and *in love*, all the different easy paths became clear and visible to me. The easy paths, in fact, are permeable. I can walk right through all the walls and straight to love anytime I desire.

I love being in love because life is easy and fun, and I am enjoying the ride.

The path you choose to love is a personal choice. Everyone finds the path of love in a different way because the journey is unique for each individual.

Life is more exciting because we don't have to live life just the way our parents did in the past, or our friends do in the present. We get to choose our own way. We get to paint our own canvas, wipe it off and start over, or change it up anytime we want to.

My nephew, Josiah Wedgewood, is an artist from Nashville, Tennessee. When Josiah sent me the art work for this book cover he sent several samples from which to choose.

Appropriately and totally unplanned, Josiah painted the book cover on canvas. He told me that I could pick and choose, and even interchange the colors, writing, and the maze choices!

Think about changing the canvas— sounds to me a lot like how we can change and recreate our lives. Every individual chooses what each of us wants our life to look like, and how we will arrange it (or at least we each have the ability to do so).

True freedom is being completely accountable and responsible for your own life. I'm sure you now realize this truth because you are incredibly powerful, wonderful, perfect, beautiful, valued, loved and magnificent!

Perhaps unlike our parents or friends, we don't have to wait or take a long time to get to the other side of the maze, closer to Love or right smack in the middle of Love.

You have no dues to pay. *This club is free,* and there are no rules or obligations. Our club motto is "feel good". We were all in love before we came here. When we each choose, we can fall back into the lap of love again very fast and easily.

There doesn't have to be pain to gain the lovely life of which you have always been worthy and deserving. You had it once before, and you can have it again, right here and now.

Some people call this lovely life *heaven on earth -- which I consider an* accurate description. You just have to believe that your lovely life is here for you. If you can let go and enjoy the ride, you will *free fall* right into love and a joyous journey over and over again.

Author's Biography

Susan's many years of study and pursuit of spiritual growth and learning are featured in her writing. One of her goals is to help the universe be a better place.

She enjoys taking care of herself through exercise and nutrition, but most of all by spending lots of time with her family. She loves to be surrounded by love. Susan enjoys living in Colorado with her husband, Ben, and four beautiful children, Samantha, Steven, Alexander, and Mariah.

Born in Chicago in 1964, the author lived on the northwest side and attended local schools. Susan later attended Southern Illinois University in Carbondale, Illinois, where she focused on psychology and social work. After meeting her husband, she transferred to Arizona State University, where she completed both her bachelor's and master's degrees of social work.

Susan worked as an advocate for people with disabilities, then in the area of Child Protective Services, followed by service in the

Department of Developmental Disabilities. She resigned from these duties soon after the birth of her second child, Steven.

Susan dabbled in counseling for a while but found traditional counseling to be ineffective in many circumstances. She wanted to better understand the link between the spirit, mind, and body.

After becoming a neuro-physical reprogramming (N.P.R.) practitioner in 1999, Susan continued to work with the bio-energetic synchronization technique (B.E.S.T.) (founded by Dr. M. Ted Morter, Jr.), and became certified as a B.E.S.T. practitioner in 2001. Sue is also certified in Psych-K (psychological kinesiology created by Rob Williams) and has been a practitioner since 2004.

With a strong background in psychology, counseling, and social work, as well as certifications in N.P.R., B.E.S.T. and Psych-K, Susan works to heal physical as well as deep-rooted emotional issues.